GROW UP YOUR EGO

Ten Scientifically Validated Stages to Emotional and Spiritual Maturity

Jeannette M. Gagan, PhD

Copyright © 2020 by Jeannette M. Gagan, PhD.

All rights reserved. No part of this publication may be reproduced, distributed, or transmitted in any form or by any means, including photocopying, recording, or other electronic or mechanical methods, without the prior written permission from the copyright owner, except in the case of brief quotations embodied in critical reviews and certain other noncommercial uses permitted by copyright law. For permission requests, write to the publisher, addressed "Attention: Permissions Coordinator," at the address below.

This book is not intended as a substitute for advice from a licensed psychotherapist. The reader should regularly consult a licensed clinician in matters relating to his/her health and particularly with respect to any symptom that may require diagnosis, psychotherapy, or medical attention. Identifying characteristics of individuals presented in case examples have been changed, including family circumstances and life conditions. Some examples are the result of a hypothetical composite of several situations.

ARPress
45 Dan Road Suite 5
Canton MA 02021

Hotline: 1(800) 220-7660
Fax: 1(855) 752-6001

Ordering Information:
Quantity sales. Special discounts are available on quantity purchases by corporations, associations, and others. For details, contact the publisher at the address above.

Printed in the United States of America.

ISBN-13:   Paperback   979-8-89389-863-7
           Hardcover   979-8-89389-864-4
           eBook   979-8-89389-865-1

Library of Congress Control Number: 2024923851

Contents

Preface vii

1. **Dismantling the "Bad Ego" Myth** 1
   Clearing the Path for Ego Growth 9
   In Summary 12

2. **How and When It All Starts: A Sense of Self for Sarah** 13
   From Before Day One and Onward 14
   Background Research 15
   The How-To of Bonding 20
   Touching and Holding 21
   Attunement Mirroring 22
   Self-Soothing 23
   Reunion 24
   In Summary 25

3. **The Ten Stages of Ego Growth** 28
   Stage 2: Symbiotic 30
   Stage 3: Impulsive 31
   Intermediate Stages: 4 and 5 32
   Stage 4: Self-Protective 32
   Stage 5: Conformist 34
   Transition Stages: 6, 7, and 8 35
   Stage 6: Self-Aware 36
   Stage 7: Conscientious Behaviors and Attitudes 39
   Stage 8: Individualistic 42
   Selfhood or Selfishness 44
   Spirituality and Religion 46
   Final Stages: 9 and 10 47

    Stage 9: Autonomous 47
    Stage 10: Universal/Integrated 49
    In The End 54

4. **How the Ego Keeps Us Safe** 56
    Defense Mechanisms on the line 57
    Psychotic Defense Mechanisms 57
    Immature Defense Mechanisms 58
    Immature Defense Mechanisms 61
    Mature Defense Mechanisms 65
    Defenses And Ego-Growth Stages 67
    Summary 68

5. **The Security of Your Growth Spiral and the Significance of Self-Soothing** ... 70
    The Growth Spiral 71
    It's Never Too Late 76
    The Inside Holding Pattern 76
    Altered States of Consciousness 79
    In Closing 85

6. **Emotions on the Move** 87
    Overview 87
    Science And Emotions 89
    Emotions Are Smart 91
    Conscious Awareness Of Emotions 92
    An Emotional Intersection 93
    Emotional Hijacking 95
    Say Hello to Your Emotions 97
    Right Use Of Emotions 100
    Anger 101
    Professional Help And Other Considerations 103
    Meditation 105
    The Enneagram 106
    Summing It All Up 107

7. Obstacles to Growth 109
The Shadow Self 109
The Shadow Comes Into Being 110
Preparing To Do Shadow Work 111
Projection 112
Looking through the Window 116
Befriending The Shadow 118
The Round Table 118
Dreams and Daydreams 121
Paradox 126
Last Words 130

8. Does Dorothy Get to Heaven? 131
Somewhere Over The Rainbow 131
Dorothy's Climb 132
What Ken Wilber Has To Say 138
What George Vaillant Has To Say 142
Summary 144

9. Amazing Grace: Scientific Convergence and Beyond 146
Self-Actualization 147
Unitive Equals Integrative 148
Vaillant Revisited 149
Peak Experience And Beyond 150
Creativity 150
The Beyond 151
Evolution Is Upon Us 152

Appendix A. Growth Spiral Images 157
Appendix B. Feeling Word List 160
Appendix C. Professional Help 165

PREFACE

Were Sigmund Freud to peek in on us today, we can only wonder how he would react to the ego's reputation, ego being the system he originally put at the very center of personality structure. Little did he know how the term *narcissism*—the overvaluation of and preoccupation with the self—would become interchangeable with *ego*. Neither could he have anticipated the extent to which the word *ego* would become as much a household word as his own name. From Narcissus enraptured with his own reflection to the neighbor who constantly self-refers, the notion prevails that the ego is much in need of extinction.

Nonetheless, I believe Freud would be gratified to know that, amid all the controversy, the ego has not only theoretically survived but has also been scientifically validated. Psychologist Jane Loevinger (1976), armed with data from thousands of subjects, substantiated ten stages of ego growth with evidence of individuals reaching the top stage. Psychiatrist George Vaillant (1993) verified the existence of coping methods of the ego—defense mechanisms—by studying the profiles of individuals over decades of time. In demonstrating the importance of these defenses to our well-being, he also validated how they can and do mature.

From a multitude of perspectives, the behavioral and physiological sciences are producing enlightening results. We have learned that results do, indeed, show that what couldn't be assuredly referred to in black-and-white terms a century ago is now being brought to us in color via very precise brain imaging. The developing brain is so astoundingly malleable and responsive to human interaction that the quality of the relationship between the infant and its caretakers makes the difference between egos that mature and those that don't. For example, parents who give their infants consistent loving care and engage in appropriate emotional responses with them provide the groundwork of trust necessary for the ego to grow. On the other hand, caregivers who display emotional inconsistency and abusiveness obstruct the foundation of security and the child's ability to psychologically mature. Yet imaging also reveals how dysfunctional emotional patterns in adult brains improve with psychotherapy. In other words, no matter our age or stage, we can grow up!

Equally significant and inspirational is the other half of this research story: the maturing ego is accompanied by a natural unfolding of our *innate spirituality*. The higher stages of growth open us to transcendent experiences, expansion of consciousness, a feeling of universality and brotherhood, altruistic acts, and awe for the sacred. Not only Loevinger and Vaillant but also psychologist Abraham Maslow, among others, show that in the evolution of humankind we are meant to know and express the truth of our souls, which contributes to both individual and collective equanimity.

The need for redeeming the reputation of the ego and affirming its relationship to spirituality is abundantly apparent. Never before has the public sought such a quantity of spiritual and religious information, including the appearance of such books on bestseller lists. People are looking for answers, not only with concern for themselves but with concern for the welfare of the planet. The valuable input science now has to offer is that growth and honoring of selfhood delivers us to the place that most religions espouse: love and care of our neighbor, here or on the other side of the world.

Grow Up Your Ego is designed to answer these issues in a focused and personal way. In these pages, you will discover five essential benefits to aid your own growth:

◊ factual information about the ego and how it grows throughout life; understanding about how your conscious participation in befriending your ego will quicken and strengthen your emotional growth;
◊ insight into how your emotional maturity is ultimately intertwined with spirituality;
◊ inspiration to commit to ego-growth work; and
◊ questions that provide a concrete opportunity to explore where you are on your path to maturity and exercises to help you move forward.

You will experience what it means to befriend your ego—to know its strengths and weaknesses, to use its capacity to negotiate primitive behaviors and downsize unrealistic idealizations, and to call forth its hidden resources. By embracing the power of your ego, you will quiet your insecurities and develop into wholeness. These goals are attainable, and this book provides a ten-step path to get you there. Specifically, each chapter guides you through a progressive network of information that directly influences how you can heal growth deficits. You will learn:

- ◊ to locate your present stage of growth; to identify ego defense mechanisms that inhibit your growth;
- ◊ the healing power of self-nurturing and how to use it in your life;
- ◊ the significance of emotions in the mind body connection and how to work with (and not against) them;
- ◊ guidelines for navigating growth obstacles;
- ◊ how to grow toward the spiritual emergence that occurs in the higher stages of growth; and
- ◊ the amazing convergence of scientific conclusions that show how the ego anchors expansion of consciousness at the summit of growth—where you will explore and manifest your truest and highest potential.

This book is not a magic potion that will deliver ultimate peace and happiness by the time you read the last page. Nonetheless, it can make a compelling contribution to your quest for emotional and spiritual fulfillment. For this book is many things:

- ◊ it is a convergence of sound psychological and spiritual information;
- ◊ it is a launching pad for growth and evolution; it is a reference guide;
- ◊ it is a motivational text; and
- ◊ it is both pragmatic and mystical.

May it generate new healing forces within you.

Ego growth is a lifelong pursuit that needs all the help we can get—from educating ourselves to psychotherapy to visiting the wise old neighbor down the street. With the right assistance at the right time, we hasten our growth.

The fact that you are reading these words suggests something within you wants to be known.

The questions and exercises in this book, whether responded to in written form or stored in your memory, offer valuable insights that can catalyze movement to the next growth stage. The following icons will help you locate and refer back to important places throughout the text.

Starred Information Exercise Review

Identifying characteristics of individuals presented in case examples have been changed, including family circumstances and life conditions. Some examples are the result of a hypothetical composite of several situations.

WORKS CITED

Loevinger, J. (1976). *Ego development: Conceptions and theories*. San Francisco: Jossey-Bass. Maslow, A. H. (1968). *Toward a psychology of being*. New York: D. Van Nostrand Company. Vaillant, G. E. (1993). *The wisdom of the ego*. Cambridge, MA: Harvard University Press.

Dismantling the "Bad Ego" Myth

Do you sit in judgment of the ego? Do you think the ego would best be gotten rid of or is too big? This book will reveal how a full understanding of the ego's essence will further your emotional and spiritual evolution and strengthen your intent to make the ego your ally. So we begin by debunking the myths that surround this part of our humanness.

Theories of psychology are increasingly subject to scientific scrutiny, with personality components being no exception. Behavioral research now shows that the ego not only is real but is also responsible for two very important jobs: it helps us survive, and it gives us a sense of self. However, the ego requires as much growing up as our bodies, minds, and hearts. When the growing doesn't happen, the ego, unable to cope with life's difficulties, resorts to detrimental behaviors and emotional mayhem. Such egos are not "bad," they simply are immature. To our good fortune, scientific data also solidly indicate that as the ego emotionally matures so does the ability to cope, with spirituality emerging as a natural outcome of this growth.

Nonetheless, the mythical "bad" ego is often viewed as a spiritual culprit. Early on in my clinical practice, I was surprised by the number of clients who came to my office bewildered by their depression despite months and even years devoted to one spiritual practice or another. I had naively figured that those who pursued such paths had a built-in constitution capable of dealing with troublesome emotions. Even more distressed were those seeking help after disillusionment with a guru. These individuals faced a dual dilemma: (1) the belief that the ego needs to be eradicated; and (2) the confusing feelings that occur when spiritual mentors who advocate such ego demise also demonstrate "big egos" themselves. Worse, these distraught individuals judged their own feelings of being disappointed and angry as undesirably "ego-bound." Such responses did not pave the way to growth or enlightenment.

Because at that time (the 1980s) research endorsing the ego wasn't well known, this was not an easy perspective to change. Clients needed to learn about ego essence, the stages of its growth, and how the ego can emotionally and spiritually mature. As psychotherapist and Buddhist teacher John Engler (1993) once said, "You have to be somebody before you can be nobody" (p. 119). This shorthand statement of how the ego must be well on its way to maturity before it can transcend its limitations is the core of what I have to share with you.

This is not to argue with the way in which Eastern philosophies speak about the ego or refer to its demise. Psychological theory and research have much to say about this important facet of our psyche that shows itself from the moment of our births. Although the ego has limitations, research clearly indicates that the ego can be transcended and that spirituality is attainable.

The following chapters will show you how your solid investment in ego growth will clearly change your life for the better, including loving relationships that support your individuality.

From the time we are born, we need consistent love and support in order to develop a stable sense of self—that is, the feeling of identity that optimally has evolved from our experiences as a separate and unique person with our own thoughts, emotions, impulses, and aims, over which we have had choice and control. In so doing, we increasingly live in accord with our true selves. On the other hand, a less optimal manifestation can develop when one's feeling of identity is heavily influenced by how others behave, think, and feel, compromising one's authenticity. The strength and validity of one's sense of self is significantly impacted by the degree to which one's infant ego was tended to and fostered, or not fostered, to grow. Consequently, it is important to learn about specific parenting styles and their effects on adult behavior, which will be covered in chapter 2.

For now, we will begin by putting a dent in the fairytale ego by considering how it was conceptualized in the first place, along with exploring stories of two individuals whose egos were derailed in the maturing process. You will discover scientific verification of the existence of the ego and of ego growth potential in the presentation of research results threaded throughout the book. And you will be reminded many times over, no matter the ego-growth stage or age, people can and do grow up their egos—and so can you!

When present-day psychology came into being, Sigmund Freud described three systems that make up the personality: id, ego, and superego, each serving important roles in making us who we are and in helping us become who we are meant to be. Understanding each of these components and how they interact forms the foundation for our work.

First, take a look at the id, that part of the personality that pops right out at birth, brimming with energy and wanting instant gratification. Totally preoccupied with body sensations and basic physical needs such as hunger and thirst (and later on, sex), the id's purpose is to keep us alive so we can grow up and propagate the species. Think of a screaming baby whom I'll call Ben, calmed by the grasp of the nipple in his mouth as he takes in the milk in quenching gulps. Then imagine this baby fifteen years later as a hormonal adolescent hell-bent on satisfying sexual urges while throwing all precautions to the wind. Here we have two examples of the id expressing itself in raw and immediate fashion.

Post-Freudian research further expands the workings of the id, supporting the observations of many mothers: that the pleasure-seeking drives of the libido are also people-seeking. In our example, Ben needs to be connected with people to physically and psychologically stay alive. In other words, while the id does provide us with instinctual and sexual energy to keep us and the species going, it also fuels momentum for connection, all in the service of survival.

At the same time, as infant Ben begins to interact with the world, the ego rises from the template of the id. Getting its juice from the id, the ego comes with partnered missions: it helps the id get what it wants (including survival); and it gives us a sense of who we are. How does it do all this?

First, the ego puts on a detective cap and carries on a behind-the-scenes operation, telling us what is "out there" and how it works. It warns us of both physical and emotional danger. A healthy ego knows the difference between what exists in the mind (nighttime dreams and fantasies entertained during the day) and what actually exists outside it (if you touch the hot stove, you will get burned).

Second, as Ben grows, the ego expands to help him perceive information so that he can think logically, evaluate, and prioritize. The result of the ego's internal work is that Ben experiences himself as distinct from others, with his own feelings, thoughts, aims, and personality characteristics. He develops a sense of self. As the ego continues to organize his functioning brain, bringing order to his psyche and facilitating realistic interactions with the world, Ben's sense of self matures and grows stronger.

To illustrate, we fast-forward to an adult Ben with high cholesterol, who struggles with demands from the id for daily doses of Haagen-Dazs ice cream. The ego reminds the id that such indulgence may not only shorten his life but also make him less sexually attractive, and thus offers an alternative suggestion: low-fat yogurt Monday through Saturday and the real thing on Sunday. Whether a grown-up Ben opts for such a choice remains to be seen.

Now, however, let's return to our little guy around age five, when the superego, the last system of our personality to develop, begins to make itself known. Mom is in the background saying, "Always tell the truth"; Dad pronounces, "Boys should have big muscles"; older sister repeats, "Quit picking your nose"; and the kindergarten teacher urges, "Color inside the lines."

Ben's superego internalizes the values and ideals of the big people in his life—an arena eventually including all of society. Soaking in impressions of what is right and wrong from influential figures, Ben absorbs their standards as well as their imperfections. He does this both because he is too young to sort it all out for himself and because he needs connection with these people—he wants approval and fears rejection. As Ben continues to grow, his superego and the ideal of who and what he wants to be pair up. The ethical rules he hopes to live by and the perfect person he wishes to be create the "shoulds and the should nots" in his head. Akin to conscience echoing voices of authority, part of Ben's growing up will entail sorting out which of those voices fit his truer sense of self and which are best left behind.

As tricky as it may seem, the id, ego, and superego are meant to work as a team under the leadership of the ego. That is why the ego is said to have an executive function. In the best of worlds, when the executive ego sits at the negotiating table between the primal energy of the id and the commandeering force of the superego, it reasons, problem-solves, and appropriately negotiates and controls how we choose to behave. As shown above, the outcome is then manifested in our sense of self.

What about a less-than-ideal outcome, though? Sometimes an executive ego goes awry. "Steve doesn't think straight"; "Katie is a scatter brain"; "Eve wouldn't know a right choice if it hit her broadside"; "Eric never follows instructions"— such descriptions are all tell-tale signs of an ego plagued by faulty thinking, poor decision-making, and improper behavior.

Psychotherapists bring out terms such as dissociation and personality disorder to describe specific ways in which the executive ego can run amuck. When an individual dissociates, conflicting impulses and threatening feelings are separated from the rest of the psyche and kept out of conscious awareness through distracting behaviors that can range from habitual daydreaming to manifestation of multiple personality characteristics. Most personality disorders result from an imbalance among the id, ego, and superego. They involve pervasive patterns of relating to and thinking about the environment and the self that interfere with long-term functioning. Examples include obsessive-compulsive behaviors, chronic passive-aggressive reactions, and ongoing emotional outbursts.

Like the pilot who carries ultimate responsibility for the path of the aircraft, the ego captains the ship of our individual selves. But the id and the superego, although often operating outside of awareness, are not asleep at the wheel as we steer through our daily routines. Without our knowing, their energy relentlessly pressures us, trying to get our attention to turn this way or that in accordance with their varying designs. When the superego seizes control, the critical voices in our heads compulsively drive our behaviors, leaving us out of touch with ourselves and those around us. When unbridled id energy erupts, risky sex or rampant rage can turn our worlds upside down and even put our lives in jeopardy.

Obviously, the ego has a vital job to fulfill. Yet the business of growing up a healthy ego doesn't come with tidy charts by which to measure progress. In the physical world, being five feet tall means being five feet tall everywhere.

In the psychological world, being calm and composed in a stressful work situation may not translate into the same kind of equanimity at home with the kids. The uneven course and often ambiguous nature of emotional maturing provides us all with challenges.

Nonetheless, indicators of progress do exist, and fortunately, the ten stages of ego growth (see chapter 3) now provide us with a solid measure of assessment. For instance, the individual living at the stage four level of ego growth is fraught with concerns about what others will think, doing the proper thing, and having the right stuff, while the person advanced to stage seven proceeds from a place of inner awareness and gauges achievement from self-set standards and goals.

Exercise 1.a

Each of the following scenarios demonstrates different behaviors and attitudes. Circle each behavior or attitude in the scenario and identify whether it reflects the influence of the id or of the superego. Then write a brief sentence about how a healthy ego might negotiate a more mature outcome.

1. When Ben is bullied by another junior-high student, Ben immediately engages in a physical fight.

2. Due to his military father's urging, adult Ben decides to join the Army even though he very much wants to go to law school.
3. Ben's sister Jane, known for her high IQ, spends all her spare time studying because her English teacher repeatedly tells her it is imperative she make straight As. Secretly, Jane longs to join the field hockey team.
4. Jane soothes her frustration about this dilemma by eating too much, particularly candy and desserts.

Exercise 1.b

Consider each of the following questions as they pertain to your life. Place an X next to those that reflect your attitudes or behaviors. Take a look around your life and what do you see:

- ◊ Are you riddled with worry or sinking in despair?
- ◊ Is there a voice in your head that whispers things aren't what they're supposed to be? ◊ Do you argue all the time with your children or constantly resent your parents' demands? ◊ Does it depress you that you can't keep up with the Joneses?
- ◊ Do you routinely snap at the clerk at the store? ◊ Do you think you are better than some, yet inferior to others?
- ◊ Do you spend a lot of time complaining about the stupidity and mistakes of others? ◊ Do you become angry and defensive when you're criticized?
- ◊ Do you measure your success by others' accomplishments?
- ◊ Do you glue yourself to the TV to block out the reality of your life?
- ◊ Do you think in terms of "us" and "them?"

In our complex society, the measure of our worth too often comes from getting the most for our money, being the best-looking person in the room, or other external recognitions. But these things rarely soothe the ache of loneliness or fulfill our quests for meaningful pursuits. They don't show us who we are. They have no lasting power to make us feel good about ourselves.

The answer is in your hands, literally and figuratively. With this book as your guide, it is within your power to reach your physical, material, emotional, and spiritual goals. If you are willing to make the commitment and do the work, you will grow in the best of ways with the aid of this master guide. It's a matter of setting your sights, grabbing hold, and focusing your intent on the challenges.

Exercise 1.c

Place an X next to each of the following statements that are true for you even if you experienced only one occurrence:

- ◊ I am able to calm myself when I feel anxiety. ◊ I have asked a friend or family member for support when I feel discouraged or sad. ◊ I have apologized to a person I have been rude to.
- ◊ I am able to set goals for myself not based on others' expectations.
- ◊ I am able to postpone gratification of my desires.
- ◊ I believe in a healthy balance of work and play.
- ◊ I'm aware that always following the "should or should not" messages in my head may not be to my benefit.
- ◊ I seek the advice of a wiser person when I have an emotional dilemma.
- ◊ I have been able to choose healthier behaviors as a result of hearing others' criticisms of me.

Frank and Julie: Different but the Same

We can all recount instances of dealing with problematic egos. A classic example is that of a young man named Frank, whose mission in every conversation was to convey his uniqueness and remarkable creative ability to others. He didn't need a drink or two to launch into a one-sided conversation detailing his talents and accomplishments. Those who believed his self proclamations were captivated by his magnetic drive to excel and to prove his giftedness to the world. From these individuals Frank received the adulation he so hungered for. Others who were bored or repelled by his self-aggrandizement weren't long for the scene. On the occasions when positive feedback and admiration were not forthcoming, he responded with anger and punishing behaviors.

Frank was born into a privileged family. His mother was an actress completely immersed in the advancement of her career. The home itself was a stage from which she promoted herself through constant entertaining and attempts to impress agents and directors. Frank's father, having given up on the marriage, traveled extensively and engaged in numerous affairs. Frank's nursemaids seldom stayed more than a few months at a time due to his mother's unreasonable demands. As a child, Frank watched his mother gain attention through her changing performances of behavior. He became his mother's pawn, called upon to entertain the circus of visitors with his cute and clever demeanor. A lonely little boy lived beneath this façade.

Julie's story reflects a different kind of ego difficulty. The youngest of four children, she was put into an inadequate daycare facility shortly after birth. Her tired and overwrought parents had little time or patience with the children.

From the start, Julie did not feel welcomed into the world, nor did she experience interactions with caregivers who delighted in her or fostered her sense of self. Indeed, she experienced countless situations in which she felt powerless and ineffectual. Lacking examples of or guidance for how to stretch her potential into resolving difficult situations, Julie became resigned to a life of limited opportunity and developed a pattern of choosing paths clear of anything threatening or challenging.

Later, academics provided a haven, since she was blessed with good intelligence and a natural ability to study. Eventually, Julie graduated from a local community college and began working as a reservation specialist for a hotel chain, a position requiring communications skills and the capacity to remain keenly focused. This first job experience turned out to be overwhelming. In spite of a helpful supervisor and adjustment of her workload, Julie found herself fighting back tears at the slightest provocation while desperately trying to cover up her feelings of inadequacy. Her level of anxiety increased daily, punctuated by sleepless nights, until she could no longer perform her job. She and her supervisor mutually concluded that her resignation served everyone's interests. Ultimately, she sank into a depression that required both medication and ongoing psychotherapy to repair.

Frank and Julie have very different stories, and their adult interactions appear, on the face of things, to be polar opposites. But what Frank and Julie have in common took place in infancy: they were not recipients of the loving connection they needed for healthy growth. Without this crucial foundation, Julie's ego turned to under-valuation of the self, while Frank's ego turned to over-valuation of the self.

Unfortunately, vast numbers of people suffer to some degree from a debilitating deficiency in their early attachments. Even the best-intentioned parents don't always get it right—they may follow the wrong advice, be inconsistent in their care, or be overwhelmed by demands and too fatigued to fully care. They themselves may have immature egos unable to cope with the challenges in their lives. Fortunately, just as research informs us of the impact of bonding between infants and their caregivers, research also demonstrates that it is never too late to correct what went wrong. At any time, we can learn the growing-up skills that will move us into healthier territory where, among other things, we effectively resolve emotional dilemmas, experience peace and calm, expand our humor and playfulness, increase our acceptance of reality, uncover fresh veins of creativity, and open the door to the sacred within us.

Our humanness is meant to be like a seedling in the soil that sprouts and grows. Each plant that flowers is beautifully unique in a field of wondrous color. Each one of us carries that same potential for growth. The human difference is that our emotional and spiritual development does not operate on automatic. We must cherish it and nurse it along. Awareness of that difference in and of itself can mark a powerful beginning.

Exercise 1.d

Each morning whisper to yourself or even shout aloud—"I can grow and I am willing!" This shifts weight from dreading the day or some event of the day to welcoming possibilities and opportunities for change.

Clearing the Path for Ego Growth

Like any good training schedule, Grow Up Your Ego follows a practical progression that you can adapt to your own pace. You decide what to take on and when to address it. By the time you finish reading this book, you will have launched or strengthened your growth trajectory from a solid platform of knowledge. You will grow while reading this book, and you will continue to grow long after you've finished digesting the words and completing the chapter questions and exercises.

In addition to commitment and willingness to change, two external features are in need of readiness. First is a notebook or journal solely dedicated to ego-growth work, along with a pen and a package of multicolored highlighter markers. Since responding to questions and exercises will involve referencing back and forth as specific issues weave through your work, you will find color coding of great benefit.

Second is to obtain proper support from someone you trust. While the discussions, directions, and exercises in this book offer support in and of themselves, you are also going to need another kind of backing— that of a being who reflects acceptance, comfort, safety, and caring to you. If no one like that exists in your life now, don't worry—there is an alternative which will soon be explained. But remember: our basic need as human beings is to connect, to share, to give, and to receive. We are not meant to be islands unto ourselves. When we dare to share our vulnerabilities with a trusted other, the intensity of hidden secrets diminishes while lessening our shame. At the same time, we create the kind of experience we didn't have in our early years— the intimacy of emotional honesty and the deepening of our sense of selves.

What are the qualities of such a support person? There are ten: Color Examples

Yellow
areas to explore more deeply

Red
areas in need of improvement

Green
areas where growth has occurred and is in need of continued nurturance

Blue
areas of strength and achievement

Orange
areas for spiritual consideration

1. Ability to listen
2. Nonjudgmental
3. Knows what it means to take on the challenge of growth
4. Not a gossip
5. Able to accept you completely as you are
6. Has experience in surmounting emotional obstacles
7. Is not prone to giving advice
8. Understands how your growth has its own pace and rhythm
9. Cares for your well-being
10. Is both gentle and firm

Where do you find such a being? Many people are fortunate enough to have friends who fill the bill. If this isn't the case for you, just skip question #1 below and begin with question #2.

Also keep in mind that you can respond to chapter questions and exercises in a formal way— writing down your responses in a journal—or by simply thinking about what your responses might be. Either choice, whatever suits you best at this time, is a step forward in the maturing of your ego.

Question 1

Who in your life would be a support person for your ego-growth program?

Contact the chosen individual in person or by telephone (Internet Skype can be very beneficial if the person lives at a distance) and ask whether they are available for support. Explain: "I am going to be reading a book that explores the concept of ego growth, and it has exercises and questions within each chapter. I want to be able to share my honest responses and what I am learning with someone I can really trust and who can give me support. I thought of you because you meet the ten qualities of a good support person." (List the ten qualities.) If that person is available, discuss the appropriate boundaries that would be of benefit to each of you and establish a convenient time for the next contact.

If that individual's time or energy is too limited, proceed to question #2.

Question 2

If you don't have such an acquaintance, can you think of a teacher or mentor from the past, even if they are no longer living? Or could you choose someone who personifies these qualities for you from history, a religious tradition, a novel, or a movie? Whoever it is, write that person a letter asking them for their support—a letter you don't mail but keep in a safe place.

(A) Respond to your letter of request (no matter to whom it is written) in the way you believe this person would, with all the encouragement in the world and reasons why they know you will succeed. Write it out, put it in a stamped envelope, and mail it to yourself. Appreciate that in some way this is your wiser, more enlightened or higher self speaking to you.

(B) Keep this letter of response you wrote to yourself. Post it where you can see these words of support and encouragement every day—perhaps next to your childhood photo. healthfully executed—can also provide environments in which you can safely share your growth process.

Obviously, for those who currently are in therapy, your therapist serves this support role. Make an appointment to have the clinician review the contents of this book to see if it is an appropriate adjunct to your healing process. Furthermore, group therapy, support groups, and 12-step programs—when

It is important to note that the subject matter in this book is not a substitute for psychotherapy. If you have been diagnosed with a mental health disorder, it is important you consult with a mental health practitioner regarding whether or how to make use of this ego-growth program.

If you are not in therapy and you experience considerable emotional distress while reading this book and responding to questions and exercises, make an appointment with a licensed mental health practitioner. See Appendix C for information regarding locating a mental health provider in your vicinity.

Your way of life has nothing to lose from attempts to improve. Your lovers, family, friends, and coworkers can only gain from what you learn and model to them.

In Summary

You now know the true story of the ego as the internal organizer of our personality that helps us survive through its ability to think logically, evaluate, and prioritize, as well as being the source of the sense of self we manifest. You have also learned how a correct relationship between the id, the ego, and the superego provides the foundation for growing up your ego.

The tales of Julie and Frank, with their differences and fundamental similarities, helped you understand how immature egos express themselves through varying guises. Consequently, equipped with the accuracy of this information, you are indeed ready to proceed. No legitimate reason exists for postponing growth. What's offered here costs nothing more than the price of the book or perhaps the fee of a library card. The dissatisfaction you've felt with yourself or with.

WORKS CITED

Engler, J. H. (1993). Becoming somebody and nobody: Psychoanalysis and Buddhism. In R. Walsh & F. Vaughan (Eds.), *Paths beyond ego: The transpersonal vision* (pp. 118-120). Los Angeles: Jeremy Tarcher.

Hall, C. S., & Lindzey, G. (1978). Freud's classical psychoanalytic theory. In *Theories of personality*, (3rd ed., pp. 31-73). New York: John Wiley & Sons.

This book is not intended as a substitute for advice from a licensed psychotherapist. The reader should regularly consult a licensed clinician in matters relating to his/her health and particularly with respect to any symptom that may require diagnosis, psychotherapy, or medical attention.

How and When It All Starts:
A Sense of Self for Sarah

Throughout much of the twentieth century, few were thinking about immature egos. Addictive behaviors, chronic depressions, emotional outbursts, and other symptoms of a poorly developed ego were commonly thought to be random occurrences, bad luck, or perhaps an inherited trait (which does occur) and not linked to an emotional cause. As much as possible, people kept such problematic manifestations hidden from view.

Even though clinicians knew better and did their best to educate, they dealt with a public that was burdened by the stigma of mental disorders and not yet ready to be informed. And in spite of the fact that during the second half of the last century researchers produced a great deal of evidence showing that the way in which parents bond to their offspring greatly influences ego growth, it was slow to gain acceptance in the lay population. Fortunately, as mental health concerns captured public awareness in the late 1990s and early 2000s, an explosion of sophisticated studies amplified and expanded what the parent infant investigators had already asserted.

What do we know today about healthy parent-child attachments? A great deal, and this chapter presents a validated and practical overview, illustrated through the story of baby Sarah, whose first days, weeks, months, and years of life set the stage for healthy ego growth, including pitfalls that place growth at risk. Whether you are a parent, grandparent, aunt, uncle, or other important person in a child's life—and even if you are not—this knowledge is relevant because it will shed light on what may have been present or missing for you. Without such understanding, you will not be able to rectify any damage to your well-being caused by faulty bonding.

From Before Day One and Onward

In years past, the fetus was thought of as a neutral being, a blank slate existing within the mother's womb. At birth, the brain was considered too immature to be aware of surroundings, and the first weeks of life were viewed as being pre-programmed, with the infant totally absorbed in eating, sleeping, and eliminating. Now we know the fetus within the mother's womb is brimming with activity and holds a template ripe for learning. Before she was born, Sarah was listening to well-chosen lullabies for her impressionable nervous system. Throughout the day, her parents whispered and talked to her with words of love and welcoming. At birth, Sarah emerged wide-eyed, displaying immediate hints of her selfhood. Looking squarely at her father as he first held her, it seemed she was connecting his voice with his physical presence.

From the get-go infants can show interest, surprise, happiness, distress, and even disgust, initiating a lifelong experience of relating to the world. The beginning weeks, seemingly dominated by the id unchecked in its need for survival, are not without clues to the up-and-coming ego, in the form of lusty cries of hunger, tears of discomfort, and yawns showing the need to sleep.

Sarah's embryonic sense of self manifests through body movements, emotional expressions, and the many other ways she tries to capture attention. "I feel hungry," "I am sleepy," or "I feel content," are not vocalizations heard coming from Sarah. Instead we hear cries and coos and see yawns and stretches.

Nonverbal signaling is a two-way street, for exchanges between Sarah and her caregivers transmit volumes about very specific individuals—Mom, Dad, siblings, babysitters, and daycare providers, all of whom carry godlike status for this defenseless infant. Each interaction with each individual carries an emotional flavor—the stronger the flavor, the more likely it is to leave an imprint on Sarah's malleable sense of self. For instance, if caregivers were to habitually ignore Sarah's cries of distress, she would learn she cannot expect to have her needs met, and her ability to trust would be damaged. Without trust, development of her emotional life and growth of her ego will also be greatly impaired.

Exercise 2.a

Reflect on these questions and write them down if you like. You may want to refer back to them later during your work on the ten stages of ego growth.

- ◊ What do you know about your welcoming into the world?
- ◊ Was yours an "easy" birth?
- ◊ Who was present?
- ◊ What was your first home environment?
- ◊ Who took care of you?
- ◊ How were you fed?
- ◊ Did you sleep well?

Background Research

Some parents and children just seem to fit together, others work hard at it. Some folks plan and prepare for parenthood, others become parents by accident and are not willing or ready to deal with the challenges. Some pour their all into being informed and loving, others give just a part of themselves. Some still believe that children are best seen and not heard. Some probably wonder if a wild gene from Great-grandpa Harry got into the mix. Some spend little time with their children. Some are outright abusive.

Our understanding of parent-infant dynamics is based upon years of research. According to historian/researcher Robert Karen (1994), in the 1940s psychoanalyst Renee Spitz observed infants who were separated from their mothers while in the hospital for several months, studying them through the lens of a movie camera. The raw, flickering footage he then showed physicians upset them tremendously, as they watched smiling, emotionally interactive infants become depressed, unresponsive, and seemingly filled with terror. As time passed, in addition to physical wasting, the babies were overcome by hopelessness. Confined to a sterile hospital environment with little or no emotional interaction with mothering figures, the infants deteriorated into a state of apathy and emotional withdrawal—they no longer made eye contact and no longer engaged in play. These infants harbored an unspeakable grief expressed only in thin and hollow wails. Unfortunately, when reunited with their mothers, only some of these infants recovered.

Spitz not only showed that both physical and psychological growth are dependent on loving and consistent social interaction, his sobering findings ultimately sparked a cascade of outstanding research. In the 1950s, another psychoanalyst and maternal-deprivation researcher, John Bowlby, popularized the term *attachment* to describe the connection between mother and infant. Collecting data from numerous countries, he found striking similarities across populations in the behavior of school-aged children who had been separated from their mothers in infancy: concentration difficulties, poor grades, lying and stealing, superficial relationships with few friends, no capacity for deep emotion, and lack of empathy. Bowlby believed attachment is akin to love and that our future mental health is determined by the degree of commitment brought to this dynamic process by caregivers.

Researcher and psychologist Mary Ainsworth (1978) worked with Bowlby and tested his ideas by directly studying mother-infant interactions. The assessment tool she used, dubbed the "Strange Situation," involved the observation of a stranger joining mother and baby in a room, with mother eventually leaving and then returning. Ainsworth identified three categories of infant response to the Strange Situation, with approximately 65 percent of the infants falling into the ***secure*** style of attachment (Goldberg, 2000). These babies were upset when Mom left but eagerly welcomed her return, allowing themselves to be warmly comforted by her embrace. They were accustomed to consistent experiences of their mothers being sensitive and responsive to their needs.

On the other hand, approximately 21 percent of infants were ***avoidant***, a classification indicating infants who were upset by the separation but were aloof and showed no interest in Mom when she returned. The mothers of these infants were described as rejecting, evidenced in home studies by the way these mothers did not respond quickly to infant distress, seemed uncomfortable with close body contact, and were somewhat rigid and minimally expressive.

The third category, ***ambivalent or resistant***, signifies babies who were very upset by the separation, both wanting their mothers back and resisting them at the same time. The most notable thing about the mothers in this classification was the inconsistency of their responses. Sometimes they engaged with their babies and other times they were ignoring and insensitive. Approximately 10 to 14 percent of babies fell into this category.

A fourth category of attachment style involving infants from seriously disordered families has also been identified. Because the odd responses of these infants (dazed expressions, bodies freezing in one position, huddling on the floor) seem to lack the goal of bonding, their attachment style is classified as ***disorganized***. Maltreatment of the infant, a depressed mother, or parents who carry unresolved issues around loss or trauma contribute to this style.

Exercise 2.b

Given what you know about yourself now, which of the responses do you think you would have had as an infant to the Strange Situation?

(a) secure
(b) avoidant
(c) resistant/ambivalent
(d) disorganized

What do you know about the behaviors of your caregivers that may have shaped your responses?

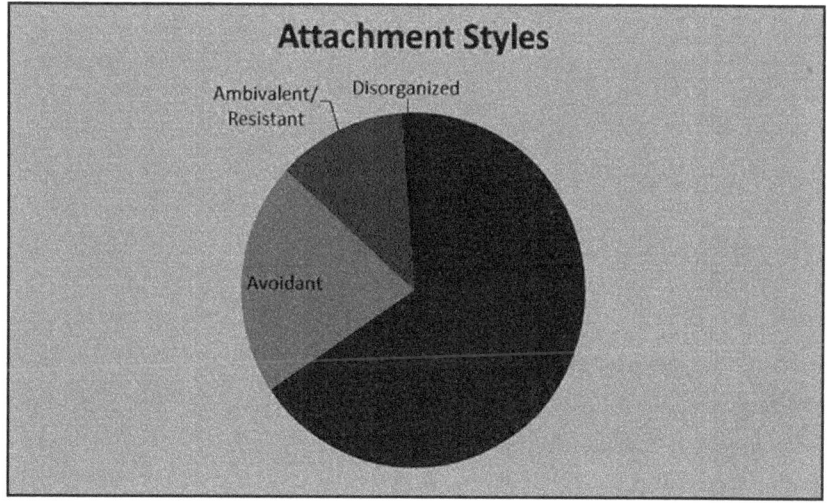

Psychologist Alan Sroufe (1983) and his colleagues carried Ainsworth's investigations still further through longitudinal studies. Armed with the data from the initial observations of mother-infant interactions, children were again assessed at various junctures in childhood. This allowed behavioral patterns of children to be compared to the responses they displayed as infants. Preschoolers who exhibited a secure style of attachment in infancy had a definite edge over their peers: they showed more ego resiliency, self esteem, and independence; they demonstrated a greater capacity for enjoying themselves; they responded in a positive way to other children; and they had more friends and displayed more empathy toward peers in distress. Furthermore, when evaluated again during teenage years, the relationship advantage of the securely attached group was still in place. These results do not stand alone; other studies, particularly of preschoolers, demonstrate that securely attached infants show more ego resiliency.

What did longitudinal studies of the less securely attached reveal? To begin with, avoidant and resistant infants did not have the freedom to explore and master their environments without worry, due to the insensitivity or unpredictable responses of their caregivers, and they did not develop the needed confidence to interact with the world in a secure way. Later on, children in the avoidant category, with their history of repeated rejection, evinced a limited capacity for empathy and often displayed anger, aggressiveness, and bullying behaviors. Resistant children, who experienced unpredictable responsiveness from their caregivers, were anxious and always on the lookout for yet another erratic event. They tended to be more passive and withdrawn and were prone to falling into the role of the victim. And how does this look in adulthood? By means of the Adult Attachment Interview (AAI) developed by researcher Mary Main, the "state of mind" of an adult in regard to attachment style can be assessed. The AAI uses a structured interview to ask parents about their own childhood experiences with attachment figures. As described by Erik Hesse (1999) in the *Handbook of Attachment*, their answers are predictive of their own infant's behavior toward them when placed in the Strange Situation scenario—in other words, history demonstrates its penchant for repeating itself.

Secure adults (related to a secure style of infant attachment) responded to the questions clearly and directly. They were able to reflect on childhood experiences, favorable and unfavorable, with understanding of their behavior and their parents' as well. They recognized the limitations of their caregivers who were supportive and the strengths of those who were inadequate. In their adult life they established intimate relationships and understood how best to relate and proceed.

Dismissing adults (related to an avoidant style of infant attachment) had less to say in response to interview questions, often reporting that they couldn't remember events from their childhood. If they conceded they had a difficult childhood, they typically maintained that it did not affect them. They appeared to be independent and strong, and presented a non-emotional view of themselves while frequently idealizing their parents.

Preoccupied adults (related to a resistant/ambivalent style of infant attachment) responded copiously during the interview. Without directly answering questions, they gave wandering narratives that ranged from vague and tangential to angry and conflicted. Details of traumatic struggles from the past often peppered their descriptions.

In sum, if we were the fortunate recipients of a secure style of attachment, we likely will enjoy a secure style with our children. On the other hand, if an insecurely attached style shaped our background, we likely will carry it forward, reenacting it in one way or another with our own offspring.

Encouragingly, however, behavioral studies indicate that insecurely attached individuals carry the potential to achieve security over time, thus improving their relationships with themselves and others, be they children or adults.

Specifically, as will be detailed in chapter 5, the longitudinal studies of George Vaillant validate this capacity as a potent growth phenomenon.

This capacity for growth can even trump genetic variants. Primate researcher Stephen Suomi (2000) and his colleagues studied how genes contribute to the bonding experience. Specifically, they discovered that when a certain variant gene (not found in all monkeys) is present and is activated by the lack of a mother, abnormal behaviors result. However, when the gene is present and monkeys do have a mother, the gene is not activated and the outcome is normal. These researchers concluded that the brain is genetically engineered for healthy development, and even when a variant exists, positive parenting stimulates emotional growth. Accordingly, when armed with correct knowledge and willingness to change, parents can repair the cracks in their parenting styles (Siegel and Hartzell, 2003).

Research results indicate how infants need to be touched, held, and interacted with if they are to grow into secure adults with a sound and resilient sense of self. Specifically, the fascinating addition of brain imaging to this pool of bonding research confirms what Spitz captured with his camera: neglected children demonstrating abnormally dejected behaviors have correspondingly abnormal brain function. For example, the brain scan of an orphan institutionalized shortly after birth shows very little activity in the region of the brain that normally receives information from the senses and regulates emotion. *This infant was not receiving necessary stimulation through touch, sound, and sight nor experiencing adequate emotional connection and interaction.* No wonder today's researchers make such definitive statements about how attachment behaviors have a visible imprinting effect on a baby's developing nervous system.

Returning for a moment to baby Sarah, consider that her brain will triple in size the first three years of her life. She will ultimately have billions of neurons or nerve cells with more than two million miles of neuronal fibers. Brains develop through the connecting of neurons, and those connections depend on the "what" and "how" of our experiences—the nature and quality of the interactions that occur between us as infants and our parents. Child development experts Daniel Siegel and Mary Hartzell (2003) in their book *Parenting from the Inside Out*, tell us: "Parents are active sculptors of their children's growing brains—we just need to provide the interactive and reflective experiences . . . which growing brains of children need" (p. 34).

For centuries in Western society, parent-infant bonding was viewed by most lay people as an unfolding process without need of attention or intervention. That stretch of time actually constitutes a dark age of infant and child development. We see now how attachment is fraught with peril and requires vigilance. Totally dependent on caregivers for nurturance, protection, and guidance, an infant's initial growth is framed by the kind of world she finds herself in. If the parental environment is hostile and rejecting, this is how she comes to know the world. If, on the other hand, Mom and Dad greet her with loving warmth, she becomes anchored in a secure nest, and the trust needed for stretching into new experiences and behaviors takes hold.

The quality of this early bonding with parents or other caregivers will shape the path of your whole ego growth. What you read in the next section will offer insight into what you may have missed "back then," while also creating a background for mending any attachment failures that may be undermining your growth. Furthermore, as you read along, it will be of great benefit to remember two encouraging factors:

1. our brains are genetically designed for healthy development, and
2. research definitely points in the direction of "earned" security and the adult capacity to emotionally and spiritually mature, no matter the difficulties of our beginnings (Roisman et al. 2002).

Exercise 2.c

◊ Were displays of affection natural in your family of origin?
◊ How has this affected you?

The How-To of Bonding

When should Sarah's parents hold her? Is there a trick to appreciating her uniqueness? How does attachment work? Won't all this attention spoil her?

When it comes to child rearing, the nuances are many, the territory vast, and the questions ongoing. It helps to remember that baby Sarah lives in the same imperfect world as her parents. Barring actual abuse, mistakes and omissions are to be expected. Babies provide caregivers many opportunities to make it right and plenty of time to do so.

Nevertheless, if Sarah is to attach securely, certain behaviors and processes are key. These include *touching and holding, mirroring, attunement, self-soothing, and reunion*—all with a necessary measure of consistency.

Touching and Holding

Skin is the earliest of the sense organs to develop in the human embryo. Ultimately, over a half million sensory fibers carry signals of heat, cold, touch, and pain from the skin to the spinal cord. Skin protects the internal body systems, regulates temperature, and metabolizes fat, salt, and water. It is also a medium of communication, marvelously illustrated by a custom found among the Netsilik Eskimo. As described by Ashley Montagu (1972), in the Netsilik culture, mother and infant communicate skin to skin, for the mother secures her naked infant (except for a caribou diaper) on her back covered by fur. When the infant is hungry, he roots and sucks on the skin of his mother's back. The mother then brings the infant to the front of her body to be nursed. When he wets his diaper, her skin picks up the sensation of moisture and she immediately tends to the situation. Motions of the mother's body lull him to sleep. Tactually the mother is in tune with the infant's needs and tends to them. He seldom cries.

Such intimacy between infants and mothers has rarely been endorsed in industrialized societies. A century ago, even physicians and psychologists were not among the wise in this regard. In 1894, Emmett Holt, professor of pediatrics at Columbia University, published a pamphlet entitled *The Care and Feeding of Children*, still popular in 1935. His advice: do not rock infants or pick them up when they cry; feed them by the clock; and do not spoil them with too much handling—surely illustrative of that sterile and dark time in infant-parent relationships mentioned above.

Today, experts strongly encourage this new parent-infant understanding: infants are meant to be held, touched, soothed, rocked, and cradled. If you are a parent and experience difficulty implementing attachment behaviors, or if you sense you depend on your offspring to fulfill your own emotional/intimacy needs, consultation with your family practitioner, pediatrician, or a licensed mental health professional is definitely recommended. (See Appendix C. Take in the moods of those who care for them is surely relevant here. When Mom is irritable or sad, Sarah takes on a worried look and tenses her body. Studies (Pickens & Field, 1993) actually show that infants of depressed mothers have more sadness and anger than others. In fact, the activity in the infants' brains reflects the same pattern as their mothers.

On the other hand, imagine Mom looking lovingly into Sarah's eyes, her gaze communicating the wonder she feels for this unique little being. Sarah takes this feeling in, and in grown-up language, the printout reads, *I belong. I have a place. I am irreplaceable.* Similarly, the cooing, singing, and soft words spoken by caretakers cushion her world, adding to the experience of belonging. Sarah's sense of self as a valued being—worthy of the effort and attention awarded her—takes root.

Attunement Mirroring

We continue now by looking down at Sarah in her crib, with the understanding that she uses our facial expressions as a way of learning about herself and expanding her brain cells. This is **mirroring**, and it involves what researchers now refer to as mirror neurons (Dobbs, 2006). When Sarah sees Mom smile, mirror neurons in specific brain regions tell her to imitate and smile back. In addition to growing and connecting her brain cells and facilitating self-knowing, mirror neurons probably contribute to how Sarah learns to understand others, the meaning of things in her universe, and the development of empathy. The concept of mirroring in general and how infants As Sarah learns to sit and crawl, mirroring expands into **attunement**. This powerful dynamic is present when the exchanges between Sarah and her mom and dad increasingly become emotionally interactive and contingent. A contingent response occurs when the quality, intensity, and timing of Sarah's signal or communication are reflected back to her. In other words, her parents align their internal emotional states with Sarah's.

What parental behaviors actually occur when Sarah "feels felt by the other?" Eye contact, tone of voice, facial expression, body gestures, posture, timing, and intensity become a gestalt as moment-to-moment feelings and sensations are echoed back to her. Sarah clasps the rattle, gives it a shake, and grins.

Dad pretends he has a rattle in his hand, gives it a shake, and grins. A smile is met with a smile, a frown with a look of concern, a funny face with a funny face, and tears with soothing sounds. The effect on Sarah? *Mom and Dad are getting it. They understand what I feel. We're connected.*

As she drinks in the juice of such parental contingency, Sarah comes to know her emotions are part of the human experience, that feelings are natural, and that she lives in a world of feeling shared by others. The richness of these emotion-filled, resonant moments not only fires connections of new neural cells within Sarah's developing brain, they bring balance to her body, emotions, and mind states as well as coherence to her sense of self. Sarah is well on her way to internal integration and the capacity for wholesome connections with others.

Sadly, we know that attunement is not guaranteed. The worst scenarios— babies left to cry for hours on end, infants bruised and battered— aren't the only examples of how the budding sense of self suffers profound scarring.

Infants of mothers who are physically ill, who are substance abusers, or who are preoccupied, depressed, or emotionally fragile are often subject to neglect, inconsistencies, and harsh behaviors. In addition to the effect of chronic stress on immature brains, any infant in such a situation internalizes a message that the world is not secure enough to support her. Her mental abilities, too undeveloped to understand the facts of the situation, sense something inherently wrong and translate this into a *wrongness within the self* rather than with those in charge of her well-being. She does not trust her own experiences nor the consequences of an unresponsive world.

Exercise 2.d

Describe a time when you couldn't connect with someone important to you. What did you feel during this disconnected state? What behaviors were triggered?

Self-Soothing

It is different for Sarah. Touching, mirroring, and attunement experiences are contributing to her secure attachment. She trusts herself and the world. She feels connected to her caregivers. She internalizes her relationships with them, establishing an inner base of consistent nurturing. What this means is that Sarah's maturing brain organizes her experiences of being soothed and held so that they live inside her. More and more, as her mental powers expand, she begins to draw on the memory of those experiences, inclusive of sensory and imagery components, turning to them when Mom and Dad are not immediately present to comfort her. This experience of **self-soothing** anchors the ego with an essential touchstone for the rest of life.

Exercise 2.e

Describe a time when you were emotionally distraught and unable to comfort yourself. Begin with memories from adulthood, then search as far back into childhood memories as possible.

In The Wisdom of the Ego, Vaillant (1993) refers to self-nurturing as "the internalization of a holding environment" and shows how development of this capacity is essential in the grounding of a healthy sense of self and the maturing of the ego. For this reason you will begin exploring your capacity to self-soothe through responses to the exercises in this chapter. Furthermore, this topic will be returned to in varying ways so that, in due course, you will have acquaintance with an arsenal of resources for building a secure platform for the ego.

Exercise 2.f

Make a list of memories and images that calm you.

Exercise 2.g

Describe a time when you were emotionally distraught and able to comfort yourself in a healthy way (not through food, drugs, addictive sex, etc.). Begin with adult memories and work back through childhood memories. Examples include connecting with nature, engaging in an artistic pursuit, spending time with a supportive friend, journal writing, and meditation.

Reunion

As infant Sarah grows into toddlerhood, her security of attachment and capacity to self-soothe are put to test in new ways. The urge for independence coupled with increased mobility push her to explore hidden corners, climb teetering shelves, and topple the living room lamp. She propels herself from one adventure to another, oftentimes with reassuring checks back to Mom and Dad in an attempt to satisfy her desire for separateness and connection at the same time. Obviously, this all can't run smoothly. Sarah's curiosity and need for freedom put her at risk and create mayhem. She discovers the power of stopping adults in their tracks and confusing their plans. Her caregivers set boundaries and Sarah says *No*. As her impulses are thwarted, temper tantrums begin to punctuate these dynamics.

Her parents are in a fix, for they must balance Sarah's need for autonomy with reality and safety. Yes, you can roll in the grass, dig in the earth, and delight in the sight of wiggly worms. No, you cannot run into the street, play with knives, or turn the knobs on the stove. Mom and Dad shout or they physically remove Sarah from imminent disaster. Sarah doesn't understand why some of her "exploring" activities are acceptable—even celebrated— while others result in harsh and restrictive consequences. Understandably, Sarah feels shame.

But wait—aren't we supposed to keep children from feeling shame? Surprisingly enough, researcher Alan Schore (1994), after an extensive review of scientific studies, concluded that the disciplining experience, when properly handled, helps the frontal lobe of the brain develop a healthy, internal adaptation to negative experiences. Just as Sarah can call on a positive memory to self-soothe, she can bring to mind the memory of Mom's reaction to forbidden behaviors. She can then curb her impulsive behaviors by anticipating her caregivers' reactions to them. This is a necessary move toward social adaptation—it's time for Sarah to learn the world is not always her oyster. Not only are there dangers out there, other people have needs and feelings as well.

Notice that something else is at play here: the executive function of the ego is making an important debut. The ego tells the self about the reality of the situation (if you throw that toy one more time, Mom *will* take it away), spelling out the consequences while reminding Sarah she has a choice (if you keep the toy in your hands, you can continue to play with it). Because the connection seeking energy of the id does not want social separation, the ego's informative stance helps Sarah develop social malleability.

But this is only half of the story; the other half is about **reunion**. Soon after feeling shame, Sarah enjoys a reconnecting experience with her caretaker whenever that person reinitiates eye contact and engaging behaviors, such as talking, hugging, and soothing. These reunion experiences ease the overwhelming isolation surrounding shame and allow reconnection. In other words, Sarah learns that, while risky activities and emotional fracases may result in disconnection, the disconnection is not permanent. The links she has with others are supple.

Sarah is lucky. Her ego frames choices in an environment bounded by people who are caring, consistent, and skilled at reuniting behaviors. With predictable and unpredictable obstacles ahead, she moves in the direction of healthy social relating, orchestrating the dance between independence and connection in a way true to her ever-expanding sense of self.

Exercise 2.h

Describe an incident from adulthood or childhood that resulted in shame, followed by a happy reunion with the person(s) involved in the conflict.

In Summary

Each of us has our own story about the nurturing we received very early in life—from parental separation to abuse to erratic attention to loving consistency and interactive contingency. The budding ego, like a plant in the seedling stage that is the fortunate recipient of the right nutrients, grows into healthy expression. But when the ego seedling is denied what is needed for growth or is actually assaulted in its vulnerable state, the absorption of nurturing experiences does not occur, and the ego is stunted. Children in these situations do not know the repair of shame. They feel separate and disconnected and, like Humpty Dumpty, at risk for a great fall.

Clearly, growing up the ego is fraught with complexity. Imperfection scripts our humanness. Even for a child as fortunate as Sarah, there are bumps in the road originating from instances of parental distraction and error. While she is not spared stress and anguish throughout life, research tells us that, due to her early secure attachment, she is less likely to stumble. But when she does, her built-in resources will help her regain her footing.

WORKS CITED

Ainsworth, M. D., Blehar, M. C., Waters, E., Wall, S. (1978). *Patterns of attachment: A psychological study of the strange situation.* Hillsdale, NJ: Erlbaum.

Bowlby, J. (1951). *Maternal care and mental health.* WHO Monograph Series, No. 2. Geneva Switzerland: World Health Organization.

Dobbs, D. (2006). A revealing reflection. In *Scientific American Mind*, April- May (pp. 22-27).

Goldberg, S. (2000). *Attachment and development.* New York: Oxford University Press.

Hesse, E. (1999). The adult attachment interview. In J. Cassidy & P. R. Shaver (Eds.), *Handbook of attachment* (pp. 395-433). New York: Guilford Press.

Holt, L. E. (1935). *The care and feeding of children: A catechism for the use of mothers and children's nurses* (15th ed.). New York: Appleton-Century.

Karen, R. (1994). *Becoming attached: Unfolding the mystery of the infant- mother bond and its impact on later life.* New York: Warner Books.

Montagu, A. (1972). *Touching: The human significance of the skin.* New York: Harper & Row.

Pickens, J. & Field, T. (1993). Facial expressivity in infants of depressed mothers. In *Developmental Psychology* 29, (No. 6, pp. 986-988).

Roisman, G., Padron E., Sroufe, A., Egeland, B. (2002). Earned-secure attachment status in retrospect and prospect. In *Child Development*, July- August: 73(4): 1204-1219.

Schore, A. N. (1994). *Affect regulation and the origin of the self: The neurobiology of emotional development.* Hillsdale, NJ: Erlbaum.

Siegel, D. J. & Hartzell, M. (2003). *Parenting from the inside out.* New York: Jeremy P. Tarcher.

Sroufe, L. A. (1983). Infant-caregiver attachment and patterns of adaptation in preschool: The roots of maladaptation and competence. In M. Perlmutter (Ed.), *Minnesota Symposium in Child Psychology* (No. 16, pp. 41-81).

Suomi, S. (2000). A biological perspective on developmental psychology: Excessive aggression and serotonergic dysfunction in monkeys. In A. J. Sameroff, M. Lewis, & S. M. Miller (Eds.), *Handbook of developmental psychopathology* (2nd ed.). New York: Springer.

Vaillant, G. E. (1993). *The wisdom of the ego.* Cambridge, MA: Harvard University Press.

Weinfeld, N. S., Sroufe, L. A., Egeland, B., & Carlson, E. A. (1999). The nature of individual differences in infant-caregiver attachment. In J. Cassidy & P. R. Shaver (Eds.), *Handbook of attachment: Theory, research and clinical applications.* New York: Guildford Press.

THE TEN STAGES OF EGO GROWTH

With the understanding of basic ego development that you gained in the previous chapters, you are now ready to learn about the ten stages of ego growth. This chapter will help you find the one that best describes your current behavioral style, but keep in mind that you might initially pinpoint a specific stage and later observe that some of your actions and attitudes actually reflect a previous level. Or you might discover your beliefs and behaviors more accurately resonate with a higher one. Why is that? It is because ego growth occurs in fits and starts, often spanning more than one stage at a time. And whatever stage you are in right now, case examples and chapter exercises will catalyze and strengthen your choices for your next step forward.

This chapter also will deepen your understanding of what it means to have a mature ego. It will provide you with insight into factors that interfere with your growth, and it will prepare you to surmount the specific challenges of the transition junctures, stages six through eight. Once you reach stage nine, you will reap the benefits of the top two stages: manifesting creativity from your true essence and opening the door to the sacred that dwells within you.

The research of two psychologists, Jane Loevinger and Suzanne Cook-Greuter, verified the existence of the ego and how it matures through ten identified stages. In the late 1960s, Loevinger (1970) created the Sentence Completion Test (SCT) that was administered to several thousand children and adults during a span of three decades. This research tool involves subjects completing thirty-six sentences, such as, "My mother and I . . ." and "When I get mad. . . ." It also entailed trained evaluators to score such an assortment of responses. Because so few people reach the top stage of maturity, Loevinger's information regarding this group was sparse.

The data from the SCT show the ego to be the central organizing tendency of the personality and demonstrate how the ego conveys meaning to all its parts: self-concept; how we relate to others; impulse control; and how we think, plan, and organize. Notice how Loevinger's "parts" reflect the two-part definition of the ego that you learned in chapter 1: it functions as the internal organizer and as the sense of self that we manifest. But you don't need to take the SCT—the detailed descriptions of each stage in this chapter will help you identify attitudes and behaviors in need of change, as well as the thoughts and actions they need to mature.

As we observed with baby Sarah, new mental and emotional tasks come with each new physical stage of growth: learning how to walk fuels the drive for toddler independence; becoming an adolescent heralds a world of new exposure with all its exciting and dangerous possibilities; and crossing the threshold into adulthood asks that we stretch into a more responsible sense of ourselves. Yet the intricacies of emotional growth are never clear cut. Unlike physical growth, which follows a logical and predictable progression and occurs in stages, the "psychology department" keeps issuing notices of opportunity and challenge throughout our entire life.

As psychologist Robert Kegan (1982) points out, we are in constant cycles of reaching for a center, finding one, and letting it go as circumstances change and influence us. We may master the challenges of one stage only to find ourselves teetering in the uncertainty and discomfort of the next stage. Or we may simultaneously be immersed in the work of two stages. All the while, we can't ignore how our environments are constantly reshaping and pushing us to change. From the crib to nursery school to grades one through twelve and beyond, we experience an ongoing kaleidoscope of new circumstances and self–other relations that summon us to redefine ourselves many times over. In the very beginning, when we are embedded in family care, we are our needs. Years later when we're involved in intimate relationships, we hopefully recognize we are not our needs but that we have needs to be negotiated.

Early Stages: 1, 2, and 3

According to Loevinger (1976), the ten egogrowth stages are only loosely connected to particular ages. She considered the first three stages as automatic and necessary for the natural growth of the personality—stages we know from baby Sarah's early life experiences described in the previous chapter. They roughly span birth to the preschool years.

3: Impulsive
2: Symbiotic
1: Presocial

(For the purposes of the growth spiral described in chapter 5, the growth stages here are depicted as rungs of a spiral.)

Stage 1: Presocial

The dawn of the first stage, the ***presocial***, occurs when Sarah emerges from the warmth of the womb. Nestled into the arms of her caretakers, bonding and attachment patterns begin, with Sarah not yet realizing she is a separate being from the world and her caretakers.

Stage 2: Symbiotic

During the second stage, the symbiotic, attuning parental behaviors hopefully occur, and the infant's attachment response begins to take form (see chapter 2). Sarah eventually comprehends that she is distinct from her caretakers, her crib, and her toys. Her learning about a world outside of herself is enhanced by her increasing use of words. Realization that "this is me talking, and there is a voice talking back to me" nourishes Sarah's budding sense of self.

Stage 3: Impulsive

The emerging self becomes even more evident in the third stage, the **impulsive**. Sarah is now toddling around the house issuing an emphatic "no" as she increasingly asserts her needs and wants—independence is budding.

She is fascinated with her body, especially her sexual and aggressive impulses. These impulses actually help Sarah confirm her own identity, even though her behavior may be frowned upon and punished— something she definitely wants to avoid. Sarah also sees others in terms of what they can do for her, and her repertoire of behaviors is expanding: sometimes she is demanding and aggressive and other times clingy and whiny in order to get her favorite lollipop.

Children who remain too long in this stage are often viewed as unmanageable or incorrigible. Clearly, as they get older, their behaviors become more complex. Such youngsters think of people as good or bad, nice or mean, depending on the kind of treatment they receive from them. Unable to see how their problems are linked to their own actions and attitudes, they repeatedly and impulsively act out. They may even run away from home.

Faulty bonding experiences are a likelihood for these unfortunate children who have tremendous difficulty moving on to the next stage without professional intervention.

Review: Stages 1, 2, and 3

The first three ego-growth stages span the time from birth to preschool years.

- ◊ The first presocial stage involves the formation of infant and parent attachment styles, during which the infant does not realize she is separate from the world and others.
- ◊ The second symbiotic stage involves caregivers attuning to infant behaviors, with the infant eventually understanding she is a separate being from her caretakers.
- ◊ The third impulsive stage involves an emergence of a sense of self as the child increasingly asserts her needs and wants, including the display of temper tantrums and rebellious behaviors. Children who stall in this stage— often due to faulty bonding experiences— most likely need professional help to move on to the next ego-growth stage.

Exercise 3.a

As you are discovering, this challenging journey of holding on, letting go, and redefining does have a guide—commitment to ego-growth work as put forth in this book. You may find that you need to allot a bit more time for exercises as they become more complex and integrative.

Look back on your answers to questions and exercises in chapter 2. Identify behaviors and attitudes (neediness, rages, jealousy, etc.) in your life today that echo back to these first three stages of life. How do these behaviors and attitudes relate to the kind of response you may have had as an infant to the Strange Situation?

Intermediate Stages: 4 and 5

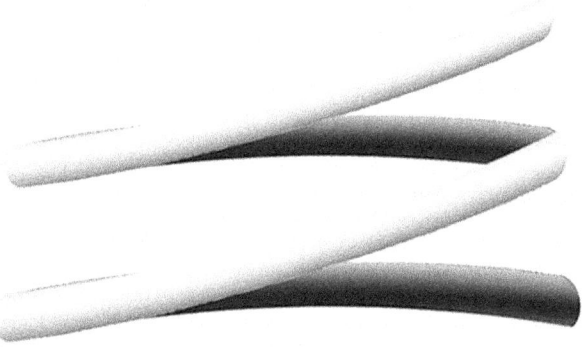

Stage 4: Self-Protective

Around the time Sarah is in nursery school, she is most likely showing characteristics of the **self-protective** fourth stage. The child at this stage understands there are rules, but the main rule is not to get caught. This is a step forward from the uncontained impulsiveness of the previous stage, and some of the benefits entail being able to enjoy rituals such as listening to the same bedtime story every night. Nevertheless, Sarah is still liable to generate disorder with her ongoing spontaneity.

Not being able to anticipate short-term rewards or punishments, Sarah and her friends are likely to grab as many goodies as they can—and blame others when they are caught with a hand in the cookie jar. While being age appropriate and standard preschool fare, these dynamics can be seen in adults. Research shows that a good number of individuals falter at this self-protective stage. Such people externalize blame onto other people or circumstances. If an individual does take responsibility for wrongdoing, she is apt to blame it on some part of herself for which she is not responsible, such as, "my hearing" or "my weight." Self-protective adults are deceptive, competitive, preoccupied with control, and view life from the perspective of "what I win, you lose." Pursuit of the "good life," with lots of money and nice things, is a driving force.

Case Study: Toby

Defensive, manipulative, and controlling as these adults may be, they are not without recourse. Early infancy and childhood wounds, when recognized for what they are, can be healed. Gradual awakenings do arise from life's accumulation of experiences. At other times, insights are suddenly triggered by overwhelming challenges, loss, or grief.

Such was the case for Toby, an individual in his mid-fifties who had spent his adult years building a small empire of retail outlets. Known for his tyrannical ways and deceptive dealings, Toby had no close friends with whom he shared himself in business or anywhere outside the home. On the other hand, he surprised everyone by his devotion to his wife, a kind woman who, with forgiving humor, put up with her husband's bullying. When she was diagnosed with an invasive cancer and died within a few months, Toby completely fell apart.

He sank into a depression that necessitated medication. At the urging of his physician, he reluctantly attended a grief support group. Here, within a room of shared sorrow, something stirred within him: for the first time, Toby began to hear and feel pain other than his own. Among other things, he thought about the many times his wife had said to him that his world was too small— a statement that, in the midst of his money-making maneuvers, made no sense to him. Gradually, in the throes of his suffering, he realized life was far vaster than his economic accomplishments, plush home, and supportive wife. He entered therapy and took on the challenge of confronting his right-or-wrong, black-or-white thinking and examined his need to have his way always be the right way. Memories of his wife played a central role as he uncovered the layers of his inner self. In his recognition of her as a flexible and giving human being, she became a nurturing touchstone for him.

Toby is a different man now, often referring to his wife as the woman who changed his life through her death. Presently in his late sixties, he is retired and spends much of his time holding the hands of others suffering overwhelming loss. Toby not only valiantly met the challenge of the intermediate stages but is now navigating the transition stages with the self-promise of continuing ever upward.

Review: Stage 4

Stage 4: Self-Protective Behaviors and Attitudes

- ◊ I tend to blame others
- ◊ My main rule is not to get caught
- ◊ One of my major concerns is being controlled and controlling others
- ◊ Competition is important to me
- ◊ A win-lose mentality directs my behavior
- ◊ I have wary, manipulative, and exploitative attitudes

Exercise 3.b

List self-protective behaviors and attitudes you are aware of in yourself. Write down your ideas about maturing beyond this level.

Stage 5: Conformist

Next comes the **conformist** fifth stage, which although loosely correlated with elementary school years, can often extend into adulthood. A significant step is taken when the child begins to identify his welfare with that of a group—the family for a small child and a peer group for an older child. In order for this to occur there must be a strong element of trust. Consequently, the child with a notable attachment disorder (such as Toby) may not become a conformist, slipping into the downside of the self-protective stage, with opportunism, exploitation, deception, and ridicule of others much in evidence.

The conformist stage involves obeying the rules because they are the accepted group rules. To avoid disapproval, compliance with rules takes precedence over consideration of consequences. Here again, we find many adults linked to this stage. Typical behaviors include identification with a higher authority, conforming to others' expectations, concern about appearance, striving to be socially acceptable, and describing feelings in simplistic, black-and-white terms (good or bad, happy or sad). It is easy to picture a teenage Sarah primping in front of the mirror, obsessing about fitting in with her friends, and taking her cues from the collective pool of teenage confusion. Nor is it out of the ordinary for middle-aged individuals to be preoccupied with mainstream consensus opinions, never questioning authority figures, whether political, religious, or cultural. Learning to think and act outside the norm are psychological tasks not yet taken on by those in the conformist stage because belonging to a distinct group makes them feel secure. They place a high value on friendliness and niceness.

Review: Stage 5

Stage 5: Conformist Behaviors and Attitudes

- ◊ I identify with and adhere to a higher authority ◊ I copy behaviors of the social group
- ◊ Being accepted by a social group and feeling like I belong are very important to me ◊ I emphasize gender roles
- ◊ I believe there is a right way and a wrong way that is the same for everyone
- ◊ I am preoccupied with appearance, material things, and reputation
- ◊ I over-value friendliness and niceness ◊ I feel guilt after breaking the rules
- ◊ I think of life and relationships in simplistic terms: good/bad, always/never, etc.

Exercise 3.c

List conformist behaviors and attitudes you're aware of having. Write down your ideas about maturing beyond this level.

Transition Stages: 6, 7, and 8

The sixth self-aware stage, the seventh conscientious stage, and the eighth individualistic stage form the link between the intermediate and upper stages. Often starting in early adulthood, this is the period when individuals begin to question external standards and eventually define their own values and ideals. This includes reevaluating personal relationships as well as political and cultural affiliations. Growth through these transition stages may involve a number of decades. By the end of the eighth stage, the conflict between the desire for intimate connection and the need for individual expression is well on the way to resolution. But how many reach the end of the eighth stage?

8: Individualistic
7: Conscientious
6: Self-Aware

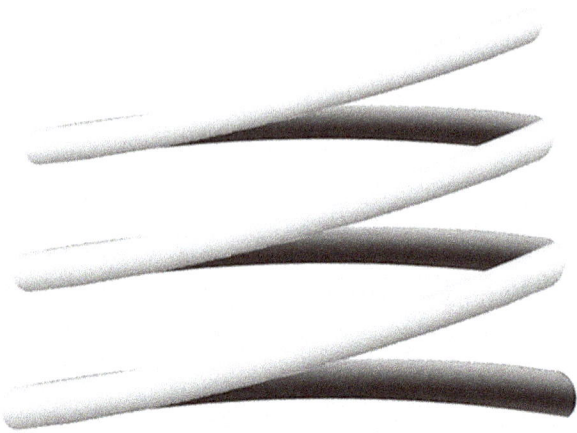

Interestingly, research indicates that 80 percent of Americans dwell in stages five through seven—the previously discussed conformist fifth stage along with the sixth self-aware and seventh conscientious stages. Why? Many reasons keep us caught in these stages: one brand of conformity replaces another, taking responsibility for what beckons seems too burdensome, and staying with the familiar is much more comfortable than the perils of change. Not everyone braves the journey through the higher levels. Yet here you are, drinking in information that beckons you to self-mastery, fortified by the knowledge that you can overcome the obstacles that previously blocked you. Perhaps even more gratifying is knowing that whatever choices you make or actions you take to transform yourself become a model for those you meet who also pursue emotional and spiritual maturity.

Stage 6: Self-Aware

Although many characteristics of the conformist stage remain active, the sixth stage involves increasing self-awareness on both thinking and feeling levels. A vague yet growing sense of an inner life triggers questions and discernment about existence, relationships, and patterns. For example, when Sarah wakes up one day gripped by the realization of how bored she is with her friends, she becomes more observant of their conversations and actions. Noting in her journal the limitations of their conforming opinions and behaviors, she compares them to students at a nearby school for international studies. Differences between the two groups astonish her, and she begins to think about various possibilities in daily situations and how exceptions to rules may sometimes be appropriate. In experimenting with alternatives, she interacts with one of the international students only to experience sadness that, at age twenty-two, her life is not as meaningful and expressive as she would like it to be.

Sarah commits to improving herself, and her journal entries increasingly describe new, more mature behaviors and attitudes. The sentiments that spill onto the page range from surprise to pleasure, from disgust to curiosity, and from alarm to hope. Although she continues to base judgments on status— whether someone is single or married, well-educated or not—she is well on her way to valuing the significance of individual traits. Warming to the glimmer of new thoughts and feelings, Sarah realizes she can no longer robotically live up to the religious and cultural standards and ideals imposed on her. And she knows that self-responsibility for her beliefs and actions comes with this territory.

Exercise 3.e

Spend two days observing when and if you appreciate multiple possibilities in situations as they occur. Ask yourself:

- What varying alternatives or possibilities might exist in these observed situations?
- In what kind of situations do I judge others based on status rather than individual traits?

Review: Stage 6 Stage 7: Conscientious Stage 6: Self-Aware Behaviors And Attitudes

- I am developing a growing awareness of life
- I appreciate multiple possibilities in situations
- I believe exceptions to rules are possible
- I seek out alternatives to difficult situations
- I have an increasing awareness that I am not living up to social standards or my ideals
- I have an increasing acceptance of individual differences
- I base judgments on status (marriage, career, education) rather than on individual traits.

Exercise 3.d

List self-aware behaviors and attitudes you're aware of having.

This brings us to the conscientious seventh stage, a time when lessons learned during the self-aware stage are applied. Many hover between the sixth self-aware stage and the seventh conscientious stage because this shift from group norms to self-styling one's own principles can increase apprehension and tension as routines and relationships change. Sorting out and discarding what no longer fits is painful. Transforming into new ways of being more in accord with emerging perceptions and needs is difficult and is especially so as we experience a world much different from our forebears' world, where following prescribed roles in committed relationships was routine. Now the challenge of shared gender responsibility and risks of emotional intimacy constitute far scarier fare. Contrary to what many fear— that such change leads to anarchy and chaos—the road to ego maturity is flanked by freedom on one side and responsibility on the other. A road sign for any of us passing through these transition stages might read:

CAUTION!

SELF-REFLECTION, RECONSTRUCTION,

AND MORE RESPONSIBILITY AHEAD

What does Sarah look like in the conscientious stage? Increasingly she experiences herself as a competent and a self-respecting individual. She shows major elements of an adult conscience, which include having long- term goals and ideals, the ability to evaluate herself in a healthy way (in contrast to self- rejection), and a sense of responsibility that result in new personal rules to live by. Markedly—and certainly a growth advance from earlier stages—she sees herself with an individual sense of choice and the originator of how her life unfolds. Making efficient use of time, Sarah wants to know why things are the way they are and holds a strong belief in progress.

Sarah's relationships are more mutual and democratic, and they are accepted as multifaceted. Experiencing many feelings and possibilities, she views behaviors not just in terms of actions but also in terms of patterns, traits, and motives. In relationships, she holds herself and others accountable not so much for breaking a rule but for hurting another person. To illustrate, if Sarah were a Catholic questioning Church dogma, she might decide that, under certain conditions, abortion is ethically sound. Coming to that conclusion could involve immense struggle against parental and Church injunctions, accompanied by intense feeling states. If she were not yet ready to frame this experience in a self-responsible way, Sarah might project blame onto the outside world: it's all the priests' fault because they haven't stood up to the Pope, or it's my parents' fault for not seeing both sides of the picture, and so on. However, Sarah at the conscientious stage is more accepting of individual differences and the existence of alternatives in any situation. Whether her parents agree with her or not, she increasingly realizes she is different from her parents and has the ability to formulate her own opinions and perspectives. Consequently, at this level of development, realizing the sensitivity of her views regarding abortion, Sarah would experience guilt for the pain caused to her parents.

Review: Stage 7

Stage 7: Conscientious Behaviors and Attitudes

- ◊ I have a sense of responsibility
- ◊ I have developed a heightened consciousness of self
- ◊ I am committed to self-improvement and establishment of long-term goals
- ◊ I view myself as the originator of how my life unfolds
- ◊ I perceive many possibilities in situations and exceptions to rules
- ◊ I am self-critical but not self-rejecting
- ◊ I measure achievement by my own inner standards
- ◊ I believe humankind can perfect itself
- ◊ I understand that mutual relationships are complex
- ◊ I feel guilt in relation to hurting others

Exercise 3.f

Using the list above, check seventh-stage attitudes and behaviors you have observed in yourself, even if only once.

Write a description of it (them), followed by a statement of ideas as to how you can bring this attitude/ behavior more into foreground of your daily life.

The examples of Sarah at various stages of ego growth are depicted in accord with research results. But do they look like this in real life? In contrast to Toby, whose wife's death immediately catapulted him into despair, the following story of Krista illustrates a more gradual introduction to an inner life that, over time, took her from the self-protective stage to the threshold of the eighth stage.

Krista's Story

Married and the mother of two children, Krista held an enviable position as a stockbroker during the early 1990s. She described her life in these words: "I have a good husband, two beautiful kids, the house I've always wanted in the suburbs, and money to spend on trips and toys for the whole family. I work with nice people and I like my clients. What more could a gal ask for?"

Unfortunately, Krista was looking at her life through rose-colored glasses. Her sixteen-year old son Roland had a drug problem that he effectively hid from his parents for some months. Her twelve-year-old daughter Sylvia developed an eating disorder, and she alternated between periods of eating minuscule amounts of food and episodes of massive gorging behind closed doors. These dysfunctional behaviors came to light after the police knocked on the door with a warrant for Roland's arrest for dealing drugs. Shocked as the parents were, they had no recourse but to face the bitter truth. When the court system allowed Roland to go to an inpatient drug rehabilitation program in lieu of jail, Krista was greatly relieved and believed the matter would quickly be resolved. Little did she know what was ahead. During family week, when the entire family spent five days at the rehab center, Sylvia's eating disorder was revealed. Krista reeled. What was happening to her life?

What would people think? Would her business suffer? Would she and her husband lose friends? But most of all, what would it take to propel these two children into healthier patterns?

Krista developed an anxiety disorder and began having trouble functioning at her job. Spending many sleepless nights reviewing her past, she felt she was a failure on every level and especially as a parent. She beat herself up for having focused so much on material things, for sidestepping quality time with her children, and for ignoring the more meaningful facets of life.

Through individual therapy, Krista began to understand how her own upbringing shaped what she brought to her marriage and her children. Born in an impoverished family, she was the oldest of three children and keenly aware of and disturbed by the hardships imposed by an alcoholic father and a mother who held two jobs to keep the family going. She quieted the fears dominating her childhood and adolescence by looking after her two younger siblings and trying to do everything possible to avoid family upsets. She couldn't stand to see her mother cry or to hear her father stumble in the door once again with alcohol and obscenities on his breath. One thing she knew for sure: when she was grown up, she would not live in poverty and would provide for her own family in the best of material ways.

Krista learned important truths in her therapeutic work. First, she had done exactly what she needed to do as a child to survive; her intelligence and skills had served her well. The problem was that no one told her at age eighteen (as with so many of us) that the patterns she adopted in her family of origin wouldn't always work to her benefit nor necessarily match her true self.

Second, she realized the value of unearthing who she really was and wholeheartedly put herself to the task. She dug deep into her feeling states and learned how to make appropriate choices around their expression. She developed the ability to listen to and accept others as they were. Krista's husband, who eventually became worn out by the family's emotional travails, did not share her interest in growth and left the marriage, a crisis Krista was ultimately able to weather with support.

With money and material goods no longer a major focus, Krista invested in the quality of her relationships, both inner and outer. She not only moved solidly into the self-aware stage but dove into the seventh conscientious stage while also reaching for the eighth individualistic stage. Krista's commitment to facing and healing her dysfunctional issues resulted in experiences she would never have dreamed of: it opened her to an inner life; it showed her the many shades of gray that accompany life's predicaments; it shifted her focus from outer to inner standards; and it taught her the importance of responsibility in intimate relationships. Some years after the initial crisis, Krista and her children had undergone revolutionary changes—the children, grown and on their own, knew how to take care of themselves and were each invested in preventing a return to harmful patterns.

Krista's case presents an extreme example. Not everyone is met by such dire circumstances. Her story reflects how the stages of transition are truly a time when the quality of our early bonding is put to the test. Many individuals meet this test without their lives falling apart. Many move through the stages negotiating the bumps and slides by calling on the strength of inner resources and reaching out for support when it is needed. Not everyone needs therapy. Mental health information today is prevalent and accessible through various sources. The stigma of emotional troubles is greatly diminished, and many are aware of inevitable challenges we all face as we grow.

Exercise 3.g

As you concentrate on this exercise, remember that the purpose of this book is to help you move through these transitions—not only with as much awareness as possible but also with an array of pragmatic tools that temper the challenge of surprises, tone down the storms of catastrophes, and support your advance into the upper stages.

Recall a time when you were challenged by a difficult transition. Write down in your journal any factors that impeded a successful resolution. Then write down specific resources that were of help to you.

Write a note of reminder to yourself regarding these identified resources. Put a star μ next to this note so you can easily refer to it when you are next challenged by a difficult transition.

Stage 8: Individualistic

The shift from the seventh stage to the eighth individualist stage is marked by an expanding sense of individuality and increased concern about emotional dependence on others. This issue of independence versus dependence was not a major factor in the seventh stage, perhaps because that stage frequently coincides with the child-rearing years. Dealing with the question of who one is as a maturing adult—during the time that one is involved in providing offspring with nurturing, food, and shelter—often must wait. And so it does for many of us until we reach middle age, when conflict emerges between "all the things I do for those out there and all the things I never do for me."

Countless people ignore the conflict and continue in the tried-and-true patterns they have been using. For others, this period takes the form of a full-blown midlife crisis, when physiology collides with psychology as the body begins to show signs of aging and the psyche begins to brood about remaining time. Whether consciously brought forth or not, embedded in this sensitive passage is a review of one's life. The ideals we set for ourselves at age twenty-one often pale when we reach age fortyfour or more. The realization that some things will never be the same again (running a seven-minute mile, eating lots of sugar) and that some things worked and dreamed for did not happen (being economically secure by middle age, finding the perfect mate) can be very distressing. Sometimes midlife is accompanied by the onset of chronic illness and by the decline and deaths of parents or other loved ones.

In short, midlife and the transition stages can be a time of loss and grieving, dislocation and reevaluation. Common to most who desire continued growth is a sense of an internal disquiet that they cannot seem to quell, and so they move closer to examining the very foundations of their lives and relationships.

How does this struggle between individual expression and emotional dependence play itself out? Dogmatic principles no longer prevail in this quest for balance between individuality and merging. An awareness of inner conflict permeates the individualistic stage, replacing the moralism of lower stages. Relations with others intensify and may be experienced as antagonistic to the striving for achievement and distinctiveness. This struggle is both internal and external.

For Sarah, conflict arises between her roles as wife and mother and her goal of career advancement. She thinks, "If only my children were more helpful; if only the workplace were more accommodating." Yet to proceed she must differentiate her inner feelings from her external experiences. As she sees the variations and interdependence of situations and knows that context and point of view are inherent factors, she realizes at least in part how expansion of her selfhood depends on her choices and resourcefulness. This takes considerable selfreflection, tolerance of the self and others, the ability to place previous ideals in question, the capacity to problem solve and to negotiate, and flexibility. For each of us, this means we are charged with awareness of and responsibility for all parts of our lives.

Dealing with contrary situations and emotions demands balancing opposites. Sarah begins to taste the power and seeming impossibility of contradiction: "I love my children, but I don't want to give so much of myself to them." "I love how unique I feel at work, and I hate how disempowered I feel at home." Sarah's task is not easy. It will require that she let go of former self- definitions and cut through her defenses to reach deeper truths. This will manifest change in her relationships, and she will also have to face the reactions—and sometimes resistance—of those who are important in her life.

In the way she thinks through these problems and applies ingenuity to make appropriate choices, she develops the tolerance of paradox that will be honed throughout the final stages. Some individuals reach this stage earlier than others; midlife is not always the marker point. No matter when the trials of this stage are met, whether by confronting loss or by consciously reflecting on one's sense of self, we gain from increased recognition of who we are, who we are becoming, and what is waiting to be made manifest. This new self-knowledge cannot be lost.

Review: Stage 8

Stage 8: Individualistic Behaviors and Attitudes

- ◊ I view myself as a unique entity
- ◊ I understand that conflict between independence and dependence is central to eighthstage growth, and I value it
- ◊ I view conflict as partly internal and partly external
- ◊ I expect and accept that relationships will intensify
- ◊ I acknowledge the perspective that everything is relative
- ◊ I embrace the belief that context and points of view are central to understanding and thinking
- ◊ I strive to move through the dilemma of paradox and polarities and ultimately welcome resolution or acceptance
- ◊ I am interested in spiritual perspectives and endeavors

Exercise 3.h

List eighth-stage behaviors and attitudes you are aware of having. Choose one of the behaviors or attitudes you have either acquired or choose to mature into. Write down what resources will be of help to you in making this behavior or attitude more concrete in your life or will contribute to the development of it.

Selfhood or Selfishness

As you can see, the very core of the eighth stage—coming into closer alignment with the inner self while navigating the needs for intimacy with others—involves a fuller awakening to our true essence. We learn to listen to ourselves while staying present to those we care about. We don't shy away from disparities between what we require and what others request of us.

How do we balance the inner with the outer? This is thorny territory, because cultural and religious influences often lean toward serving others before the self. Self-knowing and asserting one's desires can be labeled self-absorption or selfishness. But shouldn't we pay attention to the concerns of others before tending to our own? Yes, in certain instances—parents do this every day as well as those in the service professions who put their needs aside during an assigned time of helping others.

Yet connecting with our inner selves and responding to our needs is an ability many of us must learn, especially if survival in the beginning months and years of our lives meant adapting to the ways and woes of our caretakers. If, in our infancy, we learned to keep our emotional antennae tuned to others' needs while placing our own on hold, then we likely grew up unable to recognize our own needs at all. To whatever degree we were not attuned to our needs, or to whatever extent our needs were not heard and responded to, we are apt to fall into the trap of people-pleasing. This dynamic entails denying one's true self—a person with needs, among other things—in favor of being the solution to other people's problems and needs. We "give ourselves away," often not knowing what we really want. Examples include the daughter who hides her lesbianism from her parents; the husband who conceals his awareness of his wife's infidelities; and the grandmother who takes care of the grandchildren when she is drained of energy and enthusiasm. Resentment and burnout are the unfortunate consequences of a life devoted to pleasing others. Changing such an ingrained pattern is hard work that requires self-observation, determination, and the willingness to risk behaving in new ways. Do you automatically respond yes to the many requests that come your way? This knee-jerk reaction is a danger signal. You need to learn to pause before responding. Initially, this takes extraordinary focus, but with practice you can become acquainted with "the feel" of what seems right and what seems wrong in regard to meeting demands. Eventually, with this learning comes a natural ability to say no—to assert your own needs above another's.

Learning to be assertive can be done through reading books on the subject, observing individuals who model appropriate assertiveness, and tracking your caretaking responses in journal entries. Assertiveness training is not a cliché—it is a powerful way to establish balance, harmony, and mutuality in relationships.

Recently an acquaintance of mine who holds an administrative position in a healthcare facility described his long history of taking on the requests of the many people in his life—a wife, two sons, a dysfunctional sister who was always teetering on the brink of economic disaster, not to mention all the people who depended on him for help in the workplace. "I was a basket case last year with all the demands I yielded to," he said, "trying to do and be the perfect person for everyone. I was eaten up with resentment. When I went to assertiveness training, I discovered how many other people struggle with this problem and learned a lot from the role playing we did. Things are different now. Saying no can be done kindly, with or without explanation, depending on the situation. Sometimes with my sister I give a reason and sometimes I don't, but what I've witnessed is that after her initial shock to my periodic no, she found other ways of getting things done and some of them for the better."

This man's experience indicates what happens when we tackle the question of selfishness. We develop the ability to check in with ourselves regarding how we should respond in accord with our deeper knowing. Sometimes we get a clear inner yes and sometimes a clear no. When uncertainty is the case, we learn how easy it is to say, "I will give this thought and get back to you." This not only allows careful consideration of the request, it also strengthens our ability to make time and space for ourselves and the understanding of our needs.

In Sarah's case, the eighth stage struggle between individual expression and emotional dependence was met directly. First, Sarah chose to engage with her children regarding her dilemma. She told them she was in need of more help with chores as well as in need of more time to herself. Listening to their input was of much benefit, for although they weren't keen about taking on more tasks, they were willing to do so in a limited way. Together Sarah and the children negotiated various issues with the agreement they would meet every two weeks to evaluate what was working and what was not and to renegotiate as necessary. These regular meetings produced an additional advantage since her children became more candid about their feelings and needs. As she responded in kind, new understandings and emotional connections were made between Sarah and the children as well as between the children themselves. In regard to her professional life, Sarah met with her supervisor and presented several ideas for lessening the pressure of the work environment. Although it took time and persistence, this pursuit resulted in an atmosphere that was more accommodating to Sarah and her peers.

Exercise 3.i

Recall a situation in which someone asked for your help and you weren't sure if it was in your best interest to do so. How did you respond at the time? What were the consequences? Given what you have learned, how would you respond now? Record a summary of the above in your journal for future reference.

Spirituality and Religion

The balancing act of the eighth stage between one's inner and outer worlds is complex and sometimes facilitated by experiences described as spiritual awakenings. Often clients have described such epiphanies to me while emphasizing they are not "religious" people. Such experiences bring home a truth about the self that is not subject to question—it just is. The eighth stage provides a conducive setting for these revelations because it narrows the gap between the seen and the unseen, the known and the unknown, and delivers a broader band of trust regarding our existence in the universe.

The eighth stage thus broadens emotional and spiritual perspectives, sometimes intensifying commitment to the religion with which one is involved, sometimes expanding consciousness through meditation and prayer, and in one way or another clearly redefining one's relationship to the soul. At this stage, Sarah not only would have a deepened appreciation for the meaning of religion and spirituality in the lives of her parents, but would also approach discussions regarding her dissenting positions in as loving and gentle a manner as possible.

Growing up the ego means expanding into the experiences of spirit or soul, and for many this does not involve an established set of beliefs. Their spiritual growth simply unfolds as they match their inner life with outward expression. This is tenuous territory because higher-stage ego growth takes us directly into the work of the soul that may result in ending formal religious association. By the same token, when the spiritual aspect of an established religion resonates with the person's soul, individuals often make adjustments to external dogma—remember how the conscientious stage of ego growth involves adhering to one's own personal moral code? For example, myriad are the Catholics practicing birth control who still hold fast to the sacredness of their faith.

This is not an either/or question. It is not religion versus spirituality. While spirituality pertains to the spirit or soul as distinguished from our physical nature, religion involves a set of rituals and beliefs concerning the cause, nature, and purpose of the universe. Some people are spiritual and never step foot inside a house of worship. Some people are religious and have no notion of true spirituality.

Final Stages: 9 and 10

The final stages—the autonomous and the integrated—complete the ego-growth picture, delivering us into full emotional maturity where we embrace the spiritual, whether simple, structured, or diverse. After reviewing Loevinger's ninth autonomous stage, we will diverge from Loevinger in describing the tenth stage to integrate the more definitive research results of Suzanne CookGreuter. In the late 1990s, she expanded and refined knowledge about the last two stages, introducing two aspects—the construct aware and universal stages—that replace Loevinger's tenth "integrated" stage. Even though Cook-Greuter's descriptions at times may seem abstract and difficult to relate to, the example of Sarah will help clarify these research findings.

10: Universal/ Integrated
9: Autonomous

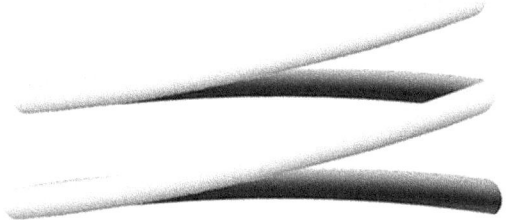

Stage 9: Autonomous

Loevinger's data regarding the ninth autonomous stage were scant, reflecting the diminished number of study subjects who reached this level. Were Sarah to grow into this stage, we would see a woman who clearly knows the ramifications of struggle, places no blame on her environment, and accepts responsibility for her life. Self-fulfillment is now more important than achievement. With appreciation for the complexity and multifaceted nature of people, she copes with inner conflict knowing that emotional interdependence is inevitable. With an increasing capacity to transcend polarities and in recognition of others' quest for autonomy, she is willing to let others, including her children, make their own mistakes. Sarah vividly expresses her feelings, including sensual experiences, distressing sorrows, and the humor intrinsic to the paradoxes of life. Personal relationships are cherished among her most precious values. With a broad view of life, Sarah stands behind universal social values and ideas, extending a helping hand to the less fortunate when she can.

Cook-Greuter's additions to Loevinger's ninth stage findings include a number of illuminating features. The goal of an autonomous Sarah is to be the most she can be. Well-balanced and definitely on the path to self-actualization and self-fulfillment, the responsibility she takes for unique mastery of her life is underlined by both independence and vulnerability.

Self-determination and a mature ego with minimal defenses not only result in integration of the more contradictory parts within her but also validate a coherent and meaningful core identity. Aided by self-insight and insight into others, she is appreciative of how individuals of other cultures are in essence like herself. Sarah believes that higher development is closer to the truth, and the more she experiences a realistic and objective view of herself and the world, the more differentiated and autonomous she becomes. Relying on rational analysis along with intuition, she evaluates, compares, and conjectures regarding possible outcomes in her continuous search for a more accurate map of human experience. Sarah is her own self-empowered person looking forward to ongoing growth with confidence and strength.

Review: Stage 9

Stage 9: Autonomous Behaviors and Attitudes

- ◊ I strive to be the most I can be
- ◊ My core identity is self-generated
- ◊ I embrace universal social values and ideals
- ◊ My perspective of the unique self as self-determined intensifies
- ◊ I value and pursue self-fulfillment, self-actualization, and self-insight
- ◊ I expect and accept conceptual complexity
- ◊ My reasoning and analysis are aided by feeling and intuition
- ◊ I increase my capacity to transcend polarities
- ◊ I integrate experiences from many perspectives
- ◊ My personal relationships are cherished and accepted as autonomous
- ◊ My higher development brings me closer to the truth

Exercise 3.j

List ninth-stage behaviors and attitudes you are aware of having. Choose one of the behaviors or attitudes that either you have acquired or choose to mature into. Write down what resources will be of help to you in making this behavior or attitude more concrete in your life or will contribute to the development of it.

Stage 10: Universal/Integrated

As an outcome of her research, Cook-Greuter views ego development as an expanding perspective on the self with renegotiation of the balance between individuation and integration occurring at each stage. This, of course, includes the tenth stage where her endeavor reveals two distinct phases: the construct aware and the universal—each involving a pattern of assimilation and integration toward a new consciousness in union with an ultimate reality. So, both pragmatically and scientifically, we have Cook-Greuter to thank for detailing what human consciousness reaches for from the platform of tenth-stage maturity. As you read on, such evidence of a reality beyond what we see, hear, touch, think, and feel initiates an entirely new realm of possibility and opportunity.

Cook-Greuter's Tenth Stage: Construct Aware

This first facet of Cook-Greuter's tenth stage describes a Sarah whose goal is to be aware of both internal and external realities. Thinking of herself as a separate individual with the mission to actualize herself, she begins to explore more complex thought structures. In so doing, she recognizes how difficult it is to be completely accurate in her attempts to reason logically and to verbally express her views. Realizing that many of her mental habits are automatic and programmed, she concludes that no matter what level of insight she gains, she will always be separate from the underlying seamless reality of ultimate truth. This includes the intricate mix of how she identifies herself accompanied by the aversion she has to conventional thinking. Due to concern of being viewed as trite or that her spoken words would be misunderstood, Sarah is cautious about sharing descriptions of herself or perceptions she has of the world. Nonetheless, her thoughts extend both beyond her own culture and her own lifetime.

In fact, during transcendent moments, Sarah welcomes glimpses into planes of reality that exist outside this physical dimension and are perceived by inner senses. Such occurrences, which arise during times of deep relaxation or while in an altered state of consciousness, often involve an opening to intuitive and creative inspirations as well as experiences of profound peace and unity.

At the same time, the limitations of logical reasoning parallel her growing mastery of paradox. On a pragmatic level, Sarah recognizes how her tendency of viewing situations in black-orwhite, negative-or-positive, good- or-bad terms is now a phenomenon of her past. Nonetheless, the construct- aware stage presents its own paradox, because the yearning to transcend ego— with its conscious thought, organizing, and planning—may be regarded as a constraint to further growth. Consequently, Sarah may grapple with the limitations of her mind as she realizes that no matter what degree of intellectual insight she or anyone else obtains, humankind will always remain separated from the underlying flawless reality of ultimate truth.

As a result, Sarah may discard the self-importance of the previous stage as she views these phenomena as insignificant in the totality of human experience. At the same time, she sees the near and the far, the subjective and the objective, juggling varying points of view in an effortless fashion. She is approaching the second facet of the tenth stage: the universal.

The closer she gets to the universal stage, the more she yearns to transcend ego and to undergo peak experiences different from all previous ways of knowing. No longer the center of her self-constructed world, she puts aside analysis and gives witness to herself as an experiencing being.

Is the ego now taking on this witnessing role? Yes, inasmuch as indirectly the ego's maturity allows Sarah to experience and to be what she is without interference. Remember that, in order to transcend, a mature ego is necessary to support travels into new levels of consciousness, including peak experiences. And without a ripened ego guiding Sarah back into "ordinary reality," where thinking, organizing, and planning constitute daily fare, she would be at risk. Emotional and spiritual instability, even madness, have been known to haunt those who pursue transcendent terrains they are not prepared for.

As you can see, linear cognitive analysis was a central feature at the beginning of the constructaware stage—no doubt a carryover from the autonomous stage of self-generated core identity. Nonetheless, as mental exploration and attempts at expansion of the known are met with the limitations of this new stage, Sarah begins to realize how the mind alone cannot provide the answers she had been searching for. And in so doing Sarah accomplishes the goal of the first part of the tenth stage: to be aware.

Review: Stage 10 – Construct Aware

Stage 10: Construct Aware Behaviors and Attitudes

- ◊ I strive to be aware
- ◊ I have the capacity to acknowledge and cope with inner conflict
- ◊ I explore habits and processes of the mind
- ◊ I know and embrace self-identification as a complex phenomenon
- ◊ I transcend polarities
- ◊ I will ultimately discover the mind alone cannot provide what is sought
- ◊ I yearn to transcend ego

Exercise 3.k

Choose one of the construct-aware behaviors or attitudes that either you have acquired or choose to mature into. Write down what resources will be of help to you in making this behavior or attitude more concrete in your life or will contribute to the development of it.

Cook-Greuter's Tenth Stage: Universal/ Integrated

To be is the goal of this final stage, as Sarah now focuses on integrative observation of ongoing experience. Perceiving human existence and consciousness from a viewpoint of universal vision, her method of knowing comes through contemplation, witnessing of flux, and the subjective experience of day-to-day life. Intellect and intuition are called upon but not glorified, as she experiences a deepening of connectedness and knowing of a deeper level of reality.

As Sarah increasingly lives in a state of ongoing transformation, she becomes aware of the illusion of a permanent individual self. Capable of witnessing life and making meaning of life's transitory occurrences in a nonjudgmental way, she relies both on her intellect and intuition. In so doing, Sarah embraces the witness (or higher consciousness) self—which does not preclude the ego engaging in its own style of witnessing.

One of Cook-Greuter's research subjects described the to beof this ultimate stage: "I am—finally in the long run—mostly unfathomable, but I enjoy the process of trying to fathom" (Cook-Greuter, 1994, p. 136).

Sarah understands the ego's tendency to objectify and concretize the self, yet she chooses to experience the self in its transformative momentto-moment changes, because her fluid sense of self is now grounded in her trust of the intrinsic value and processes of life. Choice is the key word here in relation to ego growth, for in earlier stages, defense mechanisms—with emotional survival a priority—could never allow such expansion. Now mature and sound, however, the ego can take a back seat to other ways of experiencing. Sarah knows that a goal of one's personal individuality always being the same is impossible as these changing states of awareness continually occur.

Loevinger's limited findings regarding her tenth integrated stage describe a Sarah who is most likely past the middle mark of her life and into the aging process. Pragmatically speaking, she has little company at this top stage, at least at this point in time. In possession of a consolidated identity and at peace with inner conflicts, Sarah lets go of the quest of those things she cannot obtain. She is comfortable alone or with others. She makes no attempt to change people, for she treasures them exactly for what and who they are. She engages in ego transcendent experiences that are very fulfilling to her. Sarah, now at one with herself and humanity, knows herself to be a spiritual individual committed to attaining her full potential.

Together, Loevinger and Cook-Greuter's explanations portray the possibility of new-found realizations of ongoing participation in creation, containment of paradox, peace with inner conflicts, opened doors of perception, and expansion into ever-changing states of consciousness. The exceedingly painful disconnection from self and others is forever transcended in the loving acceptance of who I am and who I am becoming, made manifest in the integration of mind, body, heart, and soul in union with the Divine.

Exercise 3.l

Choose one of the universal behaviors or attitudes that either you have acquired or choose to mature into. Write down what resources will be of help to you in making this behavior or attitude more concrete in your life or will contribute to the development of it.

Exercise 3.m

Review: Stage 10 – Universal

Stage 10: Universal (Unitive/Integrated) Behaviors and Attitudes

- ◊ I welcome a "To Be" constant state of awareness
- ◊ I participate in non-evaluative, integrative witnessing of experience and the meaning of existence
- ◊ I am at peace with inner conflicts
- ◊ I am comfortable alone or with others
- ◊ I experience a deepening sense of connectedness
- ◊ I live in a constant flux of experiences and changing states of consciousness
- ◊ I am aware of the illusion of a permanent individual self
- ◊ I rely on my intellect and intuition but do not overvalue them
- ◊ I am at one with myself and others, as an ongoing participator in creation
- ◊ I appreciate peak and transcendent experiences increasingly being in the foreground

In reviewing your lists in response to the above exercises, which stage lists your most specific behaviors and attitudes? As a result, do you intuitively identify the most with this stage? If not, review all the stages and be as honest with yourself as you can about which stage you believe is your stage at the present time.

Exercise 3.n

In reading the description of your current stage, which behavior or attitude are you willing to change? Every day for two weeks list their occurrences and what, if anything, you did to change them. Even noticing is a big step, because in the observing of them they will begin to change.

Exercise 3.o

What appeals to you about the ego-growth stage above the one with which you are now identified? Write down at least one behavior or attitude you are willing to work toward.

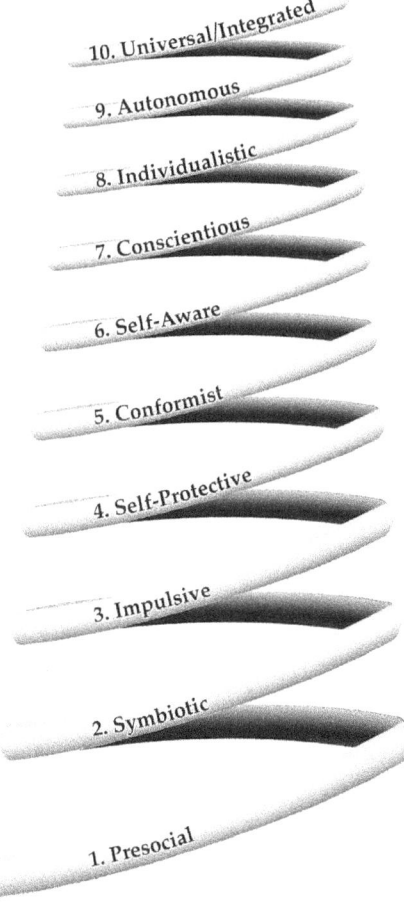

In The End

So there you have it. Does it surprise you that Cook-Greuter (1990) tells us that only 9 percent of the population advance to stages eight, nine, and ten, or that less than one-half of a percent reach the tenth universal stage? No wonder headlines broadcast such mayhem. Driven by fear and greed, self-protective and conforming behaviors proliferate in the face of differences, be they social, religious, or cultural. You wouldn't be reading this book if you didn't already know that. The difference is that you aren't squaring off with "someone out there," you are courageously taking on the challenge of confronting limitations within yourself. And, if you don't already have one foot in the higher stages, you are sorely needed there. Considering that 91 percent of the adult population score at the conscientious stage or below, millions more are needed to transform this planet. The promise of integration found in the tenth stage will not only magnificently benefit each one of us as individuals, but through united intent will shower compassion, healing, and harmony on the rest of the world. Just as the energy of fear-ridden groups tethers segments of society to poverty and malignant pursuit of power and war, so too will increasing numbers of ego-mature people expand individual awareness and universal awakenings.

So once again, welcome to the most vital, growth-enhancing journey of your life! On the deepest level, I want you to realize that each challenge you take on, each step you advance, and each endeavor you undertake toward emotional and spiritual maturity is not just for your self-mastery and enlightenment but affects the whole of humankind. Place a star µ next to this paragraph, underline it, and turn the corner of the top of the page so you can refer to it when you need encouragement, when the going gets rough, or when you would like to throw the whole growth affair out the window. As you well know from life's experiences, such trying moments are integral to any venture of merit. In fact, you may want to skip ahead to the last two chapters of this book where you will read the details of exactly how ego transcendence manifests that which is beyond what we see, hear, think, touch, and feel.

In this chapter, you have learned the stages of ego growth and read examples of how individuals overcame obstacles and matured through them into higher stages. A wide array of information regarding the critical nature of the transition stages and the importance of transcending them was provided. The nature of assertiveness, the question of selfishness, and the differences between spirituality and religion all serve as grounding understanding for ascent into the upper stages.

You probably have a good sense of where you are situated stage-wise. A later chapter will take you further into the intricacies of ego work as a spiral phenomenon and how mastering the art of self-soothing will ease and quicken your growth. But first, as you launch into the next chapter, you will discover the whys and wherefores of how defense mechanisms constitute major obstacles to emotional and spiritual maturity.

WORKS CITED

Cook-Greuter, S. R. (1990). Maps for living: Ego-development stages from symbiosis to conscious universal embeddedness. In M. Commons, C. Armon, et al. (Eds.), *Adult development: Vol. 2, Models and methods in the study of adolescent and adult thought* study of adolescent and adult thought 103). New York: Praeger.

Cook-Greuter, S. R. (1994). Rare forms of self-understanding in mature adults. In M. E. Miller & S. R. Cook-Greuter (Eds.), *Transcendence and mature thought in adulthood: The further reaches of adult development* (pp. 119-147). Lanham, MD: Rowman & Littlefield Publishers, Inc.

Cook-Greuter, S. R. (1999). *Postautonomous ego development: A study of its nature and measurement* (Doctoral dissertation). Cambridge, MA: Harvard University Press.

Kegan, R. (1982). *The evolving self: Problems and process in human development.* Cambridge, MA: Harvard University Press.

Loevinger, J. (1976). *Ego development: Conception and theories.* San Francisco: Jossey-Bass.

Loevinger, J. & Wessler, R. (1970). *Measuring ego development: Vol. 1. Construction and use of a sentence completion test.* San Francisco: Jossey- Bass.

How the Ego Keeps Us Safe

Each one of us brings a unique history to life's journey, with varying degrees of security and insecurity amid constantly changing environments. What prevents us from taking on more than we can handle? Fortunately, nature has provided us with a precise defense system— that of the ego as the observer and the protector. As we remember from chapter 1, the id's basic job is to keep us alive and connected to others, while the superego wants to keep us moral and straight. Conflict naturally results, and the ego rolls up its sleeves and goes to work. In the healthiest of situations, executive ego looks out at reality, gathers the facts, and prepares to sit down at the negotiating table between the two opposing forces of id and superego. But it is not all that simple.

Because life sometimes brings us overwhelming experiences, the ego must first of all ensure survival in the face of many odds. In this way, the ego shares an aim of the id—commitment to survival. Yet while the id operates on a very instinctual level, the ego achieves its goal through organizing, dispensing, and even manipulating information. *In this way, the ego is a master of adjustment that can bend reality so that we can continue to live.*

How does this work? The ego goes on alert when we feel anxiety and has a team waiting in readiness—a team made up of coping mechanisms that come forward to deny, falsify, or otherwise distort reality. Some defenses tackle big jobs while others are saved for smaller operations. All of this occurs outside our awareness since we do not consciously recognize a defense at work.

Suppose a child hears from his school friends that the father he adores has stolen a large sum of money from his employer and may go to jail. Realizing in an instinctual way the effect this could have on his well-being, he needs a defense mechanism so that he is not overwhelmed by powerful negative feelings like fear and shame. *Denial* comes forward, allowing the boy to vehemently denounce the possibility of his father's downfall. He tells his friends to "stop lying and never say that again," and goes about his day as if he himself never heard such words.

The full range of defense mechanisms is the topic of this chapter. In looking at the nature of defenses, you will be asked to identify the prominent ones in your coping style. Becoming consciously aware of mechanisms that automatically operate outside of awareness provides a potent handle for growth. In addition to learning about the immature ones that can be gradually let go, you will welcome the significance of the mature ones and how they strengthen your mental health repertoire.

Defense Mechanisms on the line

In *The Wisdom of the Ego*, Harvard researcher George Vaillant (1993) marvels at the ingenuity of the ego in creating defense mechanisms. He points out that, by making difficulties more manageable, defenses reduce the wear and tear of stress on our mind and our bodies. Thus, in serving as the psyche's immune system, defense mechanisms more often are healthy than pathological—a very relevant factor in today's world of high stress and unrelenting demands. What is more, this research shows no matter what our age, we carry the facility for upgrading defenses both in kind and quality. In other words, from an additional and significant scientific perspective, Vaillant's findings substantiate Loevinger's and Cook-Greuter's conclusions: it is a fact we all have egos, and with proper tending, they can and do grow up!

To understand the basic implications of Vaillant's work and how it applies to the psyche's immune system, we begin with his listing of defense mechanisms grouped into four categories, from psychotic to mature.

Psychotic Defense Mechanisms

When denial, distortion, and projection occur to a delusional degree, they fall into the first category, psychotic. Delusional means holding on to beliefs not based in reality. A person who is not able to correctly assess the accuracy of his perceptions and thoughts and makes faulty inferences about external reality (even in the face of evidence to the contrary) is said to be psychotic.

The mental health of such an individual is gravely in question, his relationships become increasingly confused, and his behavior slips out of control.

For example, imagine the father accused of embezzling goes to jail, yet the son persists in **denial**. The conversations he holds with his father at the dinner table—as if his father were present—are delusional, and the boy is seriously in need of help. On the other hand, denial typically does not fall into the delusional category. Most of us have had the experience of receiving news of an unexpected accident or death of a friend or relative. Often the first words out of our mouths are, "Oh, no," typically followed by, "I can't believe it," as the psyche struggles to take in the magnitude of the information. How such denial eventually gives way to acceptance depends both on the unfolding situation and the underlying strength of the ego, and usually it is not pathological.

While denial does not allow truth to be known, distortion twists beliefs to one's favor, although the favor may seem very odd to those of us who look on. Brenda, who lives alone and has wanted to have children, was very influenced by religious teachings involving angels who appeared to pregnant women. Distorting this phenomenon to fulfill her wish, she reported that an angel appeared and spoke about her pregnant neighbor who would soon give birth. The angel instructed Brenda to kidnap this infant and immediately move to a new location where they would not be found. Brenda began to prepare for this event by buying supplies and clothing for the infant, by preparing to leave her house, and by charting out the route she would take to the new destination—complete with arranging to rent an apartment using a different name. Brenda's warped belief that an angel appeared and gave her such information demonstrates a psychotically delusional state of mind.

Perhaps the most fascinating of all the defense mechanisms is that of projection, a mechanism that externalizes inner conflict, assigning it to other people or situations. When delusional, projection manifests in bizarre and extreme ways, such as the rage Mary feels toward her sexually abusing father—she projects it externally and believes aliens are marching across the front lawn, intent on attacking the family. Individuals diagnosed with schizophrenia frequently use projection. More often than not, however, projection is not delusional, which brings us to the next category of defenses.

Immature Defense Mechanisms

Although the term immature is used to describe this category of defense mechanisms, defenses are not correlated with specific ages. Immature defenses, which include *fantasy, passive aggressiveness, hypochondriasis, acting out, dissociation,* and *non-delusional projection,* are manifested in individuals of all ages. In this initial glimpse of immature defenses, teenage behaviors serve as examples:

- Jill, pouting about assignments without voicing her frustration and then tripping off to the nurses office with fleeting aches and imaginary pains (hypochondriasis)
- Jack, hating the macho football hero while intimidating his mother with a string of shocking words (acting out)
- Jill, floating above it all as the security guard questions her regarding the suspicious contents of her locker (dissociation) Jack, daydreaming in class (fantasy)
- Jill, harboring unspoken anger at her parents, manifested by either forgetting to do assigned chores or by haphazardly tending to them (passive aggressiveness)

Non-delusional projection occurs when the traits we dislike in others are those we don't like and can't accept in ourselves. Have you ever heard a friend talking about a person with whom she is having great difficulty, only to realize that the very quality being complained about describes herself?

Rick's story, among other things, illustrates how the mechanism of projection alters the nature of relationship between two people, even when it occurs on subtle levels.

Rick was an engineer whose work required him to spend many hours out in the field with Barry, a coworker, who talked incessantly about his material possessions. Rick was not only bored, he considered himself spiritually superior and engaged in an ongoing internal litany of judgments regarding Barry. Bringing his exasperated feelings into a therapy session, he was asked to speculate whether there was anything in his history that reminded him of Barry. He was quiet for several moments and then responded, "I'm afraid so, and it's hard to admit. In my twenties I was obsessed with having fancy furniture, a jazzy car, and the best of everything. As I say this, I'm getting in touch with what I felt then—anxiety and obsession—and I don't like it." Discovery of this hidden link between himself and Barry shifted his focus to an earlier passage in his life and the untended wounds that remained to be healed. Not only did his preoccupation with Barry lessen, Rick saw past Barry's material quest to an individual plagued by the same insecurities he had at that age. Furthermore, as Rick's attitude relaxed around Barry, something in Barry changed, and he began to initiate conversations of more substance. Without ever directly addressing the issue with Barry, Rick's inner work helped bring their relationship into more meaningful connections.

Projection has even broader implications and is probably the recipient of more press than any other defense mechanism. In an extremely influential way, this thorny defense underlines individual and collective reactions to some of life's most consequential events. In chapter 7, we will take a more comprehensive look at this particularly weighty defense mechanism.

Exercise 4.a

Think of someone whose behavior really bugs you. In your journal write a detailed description of that behavior. Take what time you need to reflect on a time or times you've acted in the same way. Record this information in your journal and place a star µ next to this description for future reference.

On a lighter note, we turn to the mechanism of *fantasy*. Who has not been carried away by make-believe delights, romance, adventure, and intrigue? Knowing this is not the real world, we soothe our tired spirits in a domain of possibility, conjuring up details of our next vacation as we sweat through the latest work assignment. Fantasy is the fertile garden of creativity, giving us an internal stage for acting out impulses in a constructive way. On the other hand, if engaged in excessively, fantasy can undermine and even destroy our close relationships and life's work. If Jack daydreams too often, his schoolwork and learning will suffer.

Hypochondriasis is the label given a person who shows exaggerated concern about physical health. Jenna, a woman in her mid-fifties, for years had pain in her neck. She was subjected to every kind of test the doctors could think of, never uncovering a reason for her unrelenting discomfort. She not only internally obsessed about her condition and its cause (a hidden cancer, the beginning of paralysis?), it was her favorite conversational topic. Such preoccupation kept Jenna from developing more intimate relationships, as well as from feeling the strong resentment she felt toward a domineering mother—a mother some would describe as "a pain in the neck." Like other defense mechanisms, hypochondriasis provides a displacement from deep feelings that our psyche is not yet ready to acknowledge.

When Ned is *passive-aggressive*, he is not able to show his anger in a direct and appropriate manner. Instead he may act helpless, dawdle, "forget" appointments, arrive late, misplace important information, or just be plain stubborn. The anger underlying the pattern may be too frightening for the individual to deal with and is complicated by the anger evoked in others who are recipients of his passive-aggressive behaviors. It *is* maddening to deal with chronic lateness, repeated excuses, or lost items for the umpteenth time, the endless rounds of such occurrences leaving both parties immensely frustrated.

In contrast, *acting out* involves uncontrolled release of impulses, usually sexual or aggressive, to relieve anxiety or other internal conflicts. Socially unacceptable behaviors such as murder and the creation of public mayhem fall into the extreme of this category, while, as shown in the preceding chapter, Sarah's two-year-old temper tantrum is an age-appropriate expression of underlying conflict.

Dissociation involves distraction from emotional pain by keeping oneself apart, spacing out, or "splitting off." A person who spends hours solving problems at the computer may be mildly dissociating, while another who has multiple personality disorder suffers a serious dissociative disorder. At the time of trauma, a person may temporarily dissociate in order to avoid the pain of an assault or wound, later described as "watching what was going on from a distance" (as from the ceiling of a hospital room or from the side of the road at an accident). To be spared physical or psychological pain at such an acute time is something we can be grateful for.

Review: Immature Defenses

- ◊ Fantasy—mental images or daydreams in which our conscious or unconscious wishes and impulses are fulfilled (often to an extreme degree or in place of engaging in real relationships and activities)
- ◊ Hypochondriasis—unrealistic and obsessive concern about physical health
- ◊ Passive aggressiveness—unable to show anger in a direct and appropriate way (being late, procrastination, forgetting, stubbornness)
- ◊ Acting out—uncontrolled release of impulses, usually sexual or aggressive
- ◊ Dissociation—distraction from emotional pain by keeping oneself apart, spacing out, or "splitting off."
- ◊ Non-delusional projection—traits we dislike in others are those we don't like and can't accept in ourselves

Exercise 4.b

Which of the immature defenses are you aware of using?

Notice if the mechanisms most familiar to you are the ones most used by members of your family of origin. If this is not readily apparent to you, through memories and visualizations, revisit family scenes and examine the behaviors you see. Write down how these behavioral examples may have influenced the immature defense mechanisms you're aware of using.

Immature Defense Mechanisms

In this intermediate category of defenses, we find *intellectualization, displacement, reaction formation,* and *repression.* A step up from immature mechanisms, generally these defenses intrude less on the lives of others than the two preceding categories.

How often do you give "good reasons" to justify your behavior? **Intellectualization**, or **rationalization**—explaining why we make certain choices or why things happen the way they do—is a favorite defense mechanism for easing disappointment and hurt. When a friend of mine wasn't accepted to graduate school on her first try, she reasoned that she hadn't applied to the right program. Focusing on that as the cause for rejection not only helped dilute the terrific let-down she felt, but also fueled motivation for reapplying to a different program that won her acceptance.

Rationalization is popular among those who enjoy dissecting the hows and whys of experience, backing up their positions with philosophical conjecture. This can keep painful feelings at bay while soothing the conscious part of the psyche.

Cartoons and comic strips provide great examples of **displacement**—the boss, who yells at his employee, who comes home and yells at his wife, who yells at the child, who then kicks the dog. It's a matter of directing one's anger and frustration at a safer target. If the man had yelled back or in some way countered his boss, he might have lost his job and the means for the family's survival. Similarly, playground bullies may be acting out their dilemmas of being picked on at home by older siblings or being abused by caretakers. When they tease, taunt, push, and shove those weaker than themselves, their sense of self is momentarily secure as they displace their anger onto targets less capable of striking back.

When we behave in a way directly opposite to our unconscious wishes, we engage in **reaction formation**. A wife, out of duty to her marriage, may play the perfect hostess with a pasted smile and sugary responses, not allowing herself to be consciously aware of her tremendous dislike for her role or the people she is serving. She uses the opposite behavior to deny her deeper feelings.

A more dramatic example is that of a shocking event that occurred some years ago in a country town. A school bus driver, described as an unusually solicitous individual always ready with a smile and a sweet welcome for each child, committed suicide by gassing himself inside his bus. This man's day-to-day behavior was directly opposite his unconscious feelings of frustration with and hatred of his life. Certainly not all examples of reaction formation are as extreme.

Repression occurs when unacceptable impulses, memories, or feelings are not allowed into conscious awareness. We hold them down in the unconscious to prevent the angst and turmoil their surfacing would bring. Take the story of the woman whose mother died when she was nine years old, saying she had no memory of the funeral or the days that followed. Years later she was told by an aunt of how she had crouched in a corner and cried for hours. The young girl forgot—that is, repressed—memories and feelings that were too painful to deal with at her tender age. Her psyche needed available energy for the growing up she had yet to do. The grieving had to wait.

Sometimes confused with repression, the defense of **regression** is not a matter of burying feelings. Rather, when confronted with scary possibilities or inevitable change, we retreat to an earlier stage of development where there are fewer demands. When three-year-old Jimmy's reign as the only child in the family is upset by the arrival of a baby sister, he may indulge in baby mannerisms, wanting a bottle and whimpering and crying like an infant. An older version of this kind of adaptation is the nineteen-year-old who, having left home to make it on his own, comes knocking on his parents' door asking for rent-free asylum. Depending on severity of the situation, regression could fall into the immature or intermediate category.

Fixation, a close relative of regression, involves getting "stuck" in a developmental stage due to fear of taking the next step. A child overcome with anxiety may hang on to mother's skirt in a sobbing clench when taken to kindergarten. Caught by the over-dependence she has on her mother, it may take weeks for her to ease into the challenge of the more independent school experience. Similarly, at a later age, a woman who is completely dependent on her husband and paralyzed by fear may be unable to take the next step toward self-sufficiency.

Obviously, defense mechanisms range in their level of adaptiveness, moving into operation when our psyches do not have the strength to withstand the anxiety of dealing with core feelings or difficult issues. Defenses brought to bear on situations of small consequence, such as rationalizing why the meter maid wasn't justified in giving me a parking ticket, may not be given a second thought. In a destructive application, rationalizing can have grave results, as when a parent repeatedly spends grocery money on casino life because of its "stress reducing effects" from a pressuring job.

In summary of intermediate defenses, consider the tale of Jack and Jill tumbling down the hill. They might have been in denial about their ability to make such a climb, resorting to fantasy about their supergirl and superboy powers. In the days before his fall, Jack may have projected his fear onto weaker males, belittling them for not having the strength to attempt such a feat. Jill may have been fixated in her role with Jack, unable to voice an intuitive hint of danger. Jack may have rationalized the importance of the journey, believing the water they went for had a better taste. Jill may have dissociated—seeing Jack tumble as if from a dream—further loosening her grip on the ground.

Review: Intermediate Defenses

- ◊ Intellectualization—justifying unacceptable behavior with "good reasons"
- ◊ Displacement—discharging tension or expressing hostility by taking it out on a neutral or nonthreatening target rather than the real source
- ◊ Reaction formation—unacceptable or threatening impulses are denied by engaging in behaviors directly opposite to our unconscious wishes
- ◊ Repression—excluding painful experiences and unacceptable impulses from conscious awareness
- ◊ Regression—returning to an earlier stage of development when threatened by overwhelming external problems or internal conflicts
- ◊ Fixation—being stuck in a developmental stage

Exercise 4.c

Which of the intermediate defenses are you aware of using? Write an example of the one you most commonly use. During the next two weeks, notice each day your use of it, making notations in your journal about different behaviors you could use to replace this defense mechanism.

Level. Instead of using our energy to defend against anxiety and distress, when we employ a mature defense we channel our energy into constructive behaviors and attitudes. Even though I prefer the term *mature ego behaviors*, for consistency's sake I will continue to use the term *mature defense mechanisms*.

This fourth category of mature defense mechanisms—**suppression, anticipation, sublimation, humor,** and **altruism**—reflects the manifestation of human neurobiology operating at its best. Said another way, researchers increasingly report the tremendous potential of the brain and its neural circuitry to emotionally and spiritually evolve. In fact, Vaillant (2008) describes a number of studies presenting evidence of how our brains, thanks to genetic evolution, are wired to obtain pleasure from altruistic behaviors.

As you read these descriptions of mature defenses, just imagine the influence of bringing awareness to the use of immature defenses and consciously upgrading them to mature ones. While future chapters will fine tune the details of this kind of growth, for now we focus on the fundamentals of these mature defenses.

Not here, someplace else

Mature Defense Mechanisms

You may wonder exactly what mature defenses are defending against. In contrast to the psychotic, immature, and intermediate defenses, mature defenses operate on a more conscious

Consider the predicament of Josie, who is going through a divorce and custody battle. She feels outraged by charges leveled against her by her spouse's attorney. Discussing the matter with her therapist, she sees she has a better chance of winning custody by keeping her cool and constructing a logical rebuttal to the charges. With the best interests of her children in mind, she decides to confine the expression of her strong feelings to two or three confidantes. This mother is using **suppression**—the use of conscious effort to put disturbing thoughts and experiences out of her mind or to control and inhibit the expression of unacceptable impulses and feelings (or both). Josie focuses on not expressing her outrage and disgust in court or in front of her children, finding an alternative way of dealing with her agitation—through a support system.

If you have had first- or second-hand experience with divorce proceedings, custody battles, or shared parenting, you know how difficult controlling one's emotions can be. Suppression is certainly not an easy mechanism to employ, but surely more apt to increase Josie's chance of winning custody. Even more important, when a divorced parent elects to forego bad-mouthing an "ex" in front of the children, the fine work of suppression helps to provide the children a better chance at sturdier mental health.

It is no surprise that experts tell us that suppression is the defense most correlated with ego strength. Learning to postpone gratification, to keep an impulse in check, or to remember the bigger picture takes awareness, determination, and practice. Yet, many succeed. For example, individuals who take care of incapacitated family members or unruly youngsters make conscious choices to hold back their feelings of impatience and frustration, while seeking other avenues for appropriate venting of frustration, such as joining a support group or confiding in an understanding friend. They also know the importance of paying attention to their own needs through satisfying diversions—a good soak in the tub, a funny movie, or whatever else replaces harmful acting out.

Not later, now

Next we take a look at Aron, who is immersed in preparations for a major speech he will give at an upcoming regional conference. We see him mentally reviewing over and over the arrangements he has made as well as the sequence of upcoming events—the airplane ride, car rental, hotel check-in and accommodations, conference room details, communications with Mr. Smith who will introduce him at the podium and run the slide projector, and finally, the rehearsal of his address. Aron is using **anticipation**—realistically planning for and tasting the emotional flavor of a future stressful event. This not only lessens and spreads anxiety out over time but also increases the chances for the experience going well. Aron enhances the anticipation benefits by sitting in his recliner and using a relaxation exercise to lower his general titer of anxiety.

Another way to do it

What do we human beings do with the id's natural instinct for safety and survival along with its incessant seeking for connection? Just as there are plentiful examples of the id's unwanted eruptions, there are abundant manifestations of the id's positive, potent energy. **Sublimation** is at play when basic impulses such as sex and aggression are channeled into acceptable social expression. A defense mechanism dear to many, sublimation is responsible for so much of what we love about the arts and what excites us about sports. Some say the folds in the flowers painted by Georgia O'Keeffe are an expression of sexual femininity. Monday night football is not just about watching a game between rival teams; it provides the opportunity to act out vicariously (resonating to the thrill of the guard who flattens the quarterback) and to exhibit socially accepted expressions of aggression (jumping up, shaking fists, and shouting). You could call it a national release valve.

Variations on the sublimation theme surround us, seasoning our lives in unexpected and fruitful ways. The charismatic preacher dramatizing his violent, drug-filled past directs aggressive energy into his appeal for reform and his zeal influences adolescents to remain drug free. Increasing numbers of women, no longer bound by the needs of their growing children, embark on midlife careers, redirecting their nurturing energy in varying ways—they may seek a college degree, enter the professional or business world, or engage in an artistic pursuit. Sublimation of energy greatly enriches our lives.

Humor at its best

Now we focus in on a teacher telling the class of her bumbling attempts to learn how to operate a high-powered yard machine. They all laugh together when she describes the outcome of a run-away lawn mower. Being able to laugh at ourselves, the marvelous defense of **humor** is not easily come by. For this is not about displacement, where others are made fun of or become the butt of our jokes. Humor delights the speaker and the listener. The orator who, at the beginning of his discourse, disarms the audience by telling a humorous story about himself does so from a place of appreciation for his humanness.

We like humor to be a frequent visitor, and we like humor that brings relief to a pressured situation. Some people have a natural talent to display humor about their behaviors while others of us set out to acquire it. From whatever source, may we each be on the lookout for our own hilarity so we grin and share it.

All for the good, the good for all

Altruism is the principle or practice of unselfish concern for the welfare of others. Illustrated in the daily ministering of Mother Theresa to the sick and poor, this mature defense enriches the giver and honors the receiver. It is not about giving with the hope of getting something in return or influencing another's behavior. Nor is it about giving to others what I myself might want. Altruism goes beyond moral judgment and beyond expectation. Countless examples never make the headlines: the businessman who daily converses with the drug addict down the street because, if circumstances had been different, he sees what he might have been; the sixty-year-old woman who joins the Peace Corps, wanting to give in gratitude for the blessings in her life; the teacher who volunteers to tutor in ghetto schools because of the sheer joy of seeing a child learn and grow.

Review: Mature Defenses/Healthy Ego Behaviors

Defenses And Ego-Growth Stages

- Suppression—consciously placing disturbing thoughts and experiences out of mind, or consciously choosing to control and inhibit the expression of unacceptable feelings and impulses
- Anticipation—realistically planning for and preparing for a future event in order to manage anxiety
- Sublimation—channeling unacceptable sexual or aggressive impulses into acceptable expressions and behaviors
- Humor—the capacity to laugh at ourselves and share this phenomenon with others ◊ Altruism— selfless giving that enriches both the giver and the receiver

Exercise 4.d

- Which of the mature defenses seem a natural fit for you? Why?
- Choose one mature defense and commit to incorporating it into your life. For two weeks, write a daily entry about how you did or did not use it.
- When you did use the defense, record the results in your journal and make note of how you could improve the use of this defense.

Suppression, anticipation, sublimation, humor, and altruism *are* the hallmarks of a maturing ego. However, once again, we meet up with the unevenness of growth: the seemingly most immature person sometimes surprises us with healthy humor, or the markedly passive-aggressive individual impresses us with her display of a timely and assertive approach. During a crisis we may rise to the occasion with a remarkable capacity for clear thought and suppression of disruptive feelings, while later collapsing into a morass of anxiety and despair. And sometimes the person we regard as mature catches us off guard with a gush of petty, projection-filled, gossip. We move in fits and starts toward wholeness.

While the mature defenses have been scientifically correlated with the upper stages of ego growth (more about this in the next chapter), the presence of defenses in the lower and intermediate growth stages is obviously more varied and less precise. Certainly, the immature defenses are evident in the self-protective and conformist ego-growth stages. Similarly, the intermediate defenses are present in the intermediate growth stages. It all depends on individual personality and the style of coping taken on in the first place: the more fragile the parental attachment, the more immature the defenses.

Furthermore, parental modeling of defenses to offspring will often produce the same defenses in the child.

Because growth of the ego involves maturing of the defenses, by the sixth self-aware and the seventh conscientious stages, intermediate defenses are hopefully more in evidence along with the emergence of mature ones, for whichever less mature defenses we grew up with, they weaken in the sixth and seventh stages. Certainly by the eighth individualistic stage, a waning of intermediate defenses occurs, with more frequent appearances of the mature ones.

Summary

In this chapter, you learned about the four categories of defense mechanisms and the individual defenses of each category. No doubt you have recognized yourself in some of the descriptions and have an idea of which defenses are specifically yours. The exercises in this chapter will help you become more familiar with your own patterns, including if and when altruism and empathy fit into your perspective. When you find yourself stuck in attitudes or behaviors that you know impede your growth, return to these exercises to help you move on.

The time and energy devoted to upgrading your defenses will be will be greatly supported by what you learn in the coming chapter: in addition to charting issues of your own growth spiral, research findings regarding the relationship between mature mechanisms, spiritual awakening, and the ability to self-nurture will amaze you.

WORKS CITED

Vaillant, G. E. (1993). *The wisdom of the ego.* Cambridge, MA: Harvard University Press.

Vaillant, G. E. (2008). *Spiritual evolution: A scientific defense of faith.* New York: Broadway Books.

THE SECURITY OF YOUR GROWTH SPIRAL AND THE SIGNIFICANCE OF SELF-SOOTHING

This chapter depicts the ego-growth stages as an ascending spiral, beginning with stage one and moving upward to stage ten. Rising up through the spiral are pillars representing issues identified as emotionally troublesome. As you learn about the points of intersection—points where the spiral and vertical pillars actually cross or are within close range of each other—the relationship between the growth spiral and your significant issues, as well as the benefits of upgrading defense mechanisms, will become more real to you. In addition, you will discover how the capacity to soothe yourself both stabilizes your spiral and furthers upward movement.

Why does the pace of this growth greatly depend on your ability to self-nurture? Think back to what you learned in chapter 2 about how attachment styles between the infant and its caretakers affect the infant's emotional development. For infants who received consistent loving attention, the ability to self-soothe was internalized. The infant was then able to call on this self-nurturing capacity when caretakers weren't available. And as you know, not all infants were the fortunate recipients of such secure attachment, the lack of which hinders emotional growth.

The ability to self-nurture calms distress and helps surmount the obstacles and challenges of emotional growth. If you have had trouble internalizing a self-soothing environment, this chapter and its case studies will surely be of help. You will learn as well the significance of mentoring experiences and the wholesome use of altered states of consciousness. Finally, you will be urged on by research results that validate what I keep reminding you of: no matter how old you are or what stage you are in, it is never too late for the ego to grow.

The Growth Spiral

The mix of temperament and environment creates the foundation for the growth spiral. What we were born with and how we were brought up varies from individual to individual, and some of us are more impacted by one than the other. Again, we know from chapter 2 that the degree to which we did not adequately bond with our caretakers produces emotional deficits that greatly impinge on how we mature and the kind of person we ultimately become.

Even in the best of environments, there are emotional disconnections and parental errors that curb full personality development. Furthermore, temperamental factors will influence responses to the environment in individual ways. A shy and sensitive child will react differently to harsh parenting (perhaps by withdrawing and being silent) than will an extroverted, outspoken child (who may actively challenge parenting behavior). Thus, this combination of genetics and our surroundings generates specific issues along the growth spiral from the ground up.

By age three, our brains triple in size, with multiplying neurons accumulating imprints from everyone and everything around us. Accordingly, imprints from early dysfunctional emotional patterning stay with us indefinitely unless we mitigate them through the labor of healing ourselves. Experts used to say the brain was fixed, and that we lose brain cells as we grow. This couldn't be further from the truth; scientists now report the brain has the power to change and transform for the better throughout one's entire lifetime. *Neuroplasticity* is the term given this ability of the brain to form new connections at nerve endings where links did not exist or were injured. For example, when a dysfunctional pattern fueled by negative self-talk ("I'm upset because I didn't get promoted—I must not be any good") is repeatedly replaced by a positive self-statement ("I believe in my potential"), new connections at nerve endings take shape, with the old connections eventually diminishing.

Because change is possible, and that is what you are aiming for, it is important to identify the core issues that rise and cross through the growth spiral, creating vital opportunities for ego maturation. The work you've done so far most likely has clued you in to several major issues, including what you learned about your attachment style, the behaviors and attitudes of your ego-growth stage, and the identification of the defense mechanisms that you use. You will use what you have learned in creating your own specific growth spiral and pillars.

The graphical image you create is important, because once we have done a piece of work on an emotional issue and experience relief and growth, we tend to congratulate ourselves for being "done with that one," believing we will never see the likes of it again. While we may well be done with that *specific* place of intersection between the pillar issue and the spiral, the fact of the matter is that we will meet the issue in new guises at other places of pillar-spiral intersection. This can be discouraging and create the impression that we have made no progress at all, yet understanding that our issues will intersect with new trials and higher stages all along the way eases the concern and motivates us to keep going. Of even greater significance is the fact that with each round of dealing with an issue, we are working from a deeper place within ourselves. With each peeling away of another layer of dysfunction and distress, we are developing new brain cells of integrative self-connection.

How do these layers show themselves? Let's take a look at Rob—an "out there" type of guy who lets you know what he thinks and feels. When he was born, his parents described his entry into the world as wide-eyed, as though he wanted to drink in the whole world. He was an impatient baby who cried loudly for what he wanted. Because of a large and complicated family situation, Rob didn't always get prompt attention. By the time he was a toddler, his aggressiveness and temper tantrums overwhelmed his parents.

Finally, when he was four years old, they followed the advice of their doctor and consulted a therapist. In addition to play therapy for Rob, the parents learned how their child was struggling within himself and how they could more appropriately manage his frustration.

The lives of Rob and his parents were beneficially influenced as their brains sprouted new neurons that changed behaviors and improved their relationships. At the same time, Rob's basic issue of aggression and competitiveness was with him for life—his unique blend of temperament and environment. When he went to elementary school, the challenge of cooperation and participation required more learning of how to adapt his action-oriented style. In adolescence, the same basic issue manifested through his rebellious tendencies. Further down the line, in a committed relationship, he met a whole new territory of needs and demands. We can hope that Rob will keep his aggressive nature appropriately in check by learning mature ego defense mechanisms (such as sublimation and suppression) that promote the formation of healthier neural imprints.

Figure 1 (page 62) shows a replica of a spiral drawn by a forty-five year old client, Natalie, to illustrate her ego growth and how troubling issues in her life intersected and affected her progress. Notice how the four vertical lines intersecting the spiral each have an "issue label"—issues identified in her therapy process. Notice also how these vertical lines intersect between ego-growth stages five and six, since Natalie pinpointed her ego-growth stage somewhere between conformity and self-awareness. Fearful that her live-in boyfriend would leave, Natalie described a pattern of serial partnerships that never lasted more than a year or two. As therapy unfolded, Natalie learned that the avoidant style best illustrated the kind of attachment she had with her mother.

Her desire for close emotional relationships was thwarted by her inability to share feelings or to engage in spontaneous behaviors. She tended to withdraw when others expressed strong emotions and admitted that she herself rarely felt angry and had not truly grieved the loss of previous relationships or the recent death of her dearly loved dog. She came up with four pillars that she labeled as lack of trust, fear of change, emotional disconnectedness, and unprocessed grief. Obviously, there is overlap among these issues, and repression can be seen as a major defense. Through therapy, Natalie came to understand that if she had been more in touch with her emotions, she would have grieved when she needed to. If she felt trusting of herself and the world, she would not have had as much fear of change. She decided that sticking with therapy was a beneficial way to work on her issue of trust.

A. Lack of trust
B. Fear of change
C. Emotional disconnectedness D. Unprocessed grief

Figure 1: *Growth spiral with intersecting pillars*

Her next priority involved examining her emotional life, because the common complaint of all her partners (present and past) was that she was "too clammed up." Natalie worked hard, making a potent advance when she agreed to attend group therapy. A reactivation of her major issues resulted— another junction on the spiral. However, the progress made in individual therapy buoyed her through this new test, promoting the deepening of trust and the daring of new behaviors. I suspect if Natalie were to redraw the spiral today she would add more issues. However, the four she established at the beginning provided the jump-start she needed to redirect her psyche and to make acquaintance with the invitations issuing from her more trusting self.

And so it will be as any of us move up life's spiral. Ongoing events and trials will put our basic issues to the test many times over. At the same time, the successes we have accrued will guide us—new neural connections help us remember that our emotional health is so much greater than before. It is a matter of stopping to recall what contributed to resolution of a specific dilemma when it previously hit the spiral intersection and then putting it to use once again along with the use of mature defense mechanisms. By the time any of us reaches the top stages of ego growth, we will not only be more accepting of our basic issues but also more adept handlers of their tricks and guises.

Exercise 5.a

In your journal, draw your own growth spiral or copy the image as illustrated in Appendix A. (A simple way to do this is to draw a continuous, wide "S.")

Referring back to Exercise 3.m (chapter 3), identify your current stage of growth and mark the spiral at that stage with a star μ.

Now dissect the spiral with a line (a pillar) representing each issue, temperamental or environmental, that you can identify. In particular, review Exercises 3.b, 3.c, 3.d, 3.f, and 3.n.

Write a paragraph describing each issue. At the end of each paragraph, list the defense mechanism you most commonly use with the issues. Put a star μ next to the most problematic issue and write down how you are working on it.

If you are not working on it, write down ideas about how you could begin, including upgrading the defense to a more mature defense mechanism.

It's Never Too Late

What about the evidence that it is never too late to grow up the ego? Beginning as early as 1910, three longitudinal studies evaluated more than 2,000 subjects at specific intervals throughout their lives. Over a multitude of decades, investigators carefully recorded responses to interview questions, studied answers to written questionnaires, and collected baseline data to assess how these individuals coped with difficulties. Analysis of the results confirmed how an impressive number of subjects changed their ways of coping over time through maturing their defense mechanisms.

Vaillant (1993) examined the results of these studies and reached several important conclusions. First, specific defense mechanisms are real and can be measured. Projection, denial, suppression, and all the other defenses we learned about in chapter 4 are tangible dynamics that provide a great deal of information about our personalities in the way we operate within ourselves and in the presence of others.

Second, because various psychological tests had been used, Vaillant was able to establish that the most mature ego defenses were found in those individuals who had attained the highest degree of psychological adjustment. Furthermore, it did not matter what social class, which gender, or how much education the subjects had—the more mature their defenses, the better their mental health. Anatomy, behavior, and physiology, on the other hand, negatively impacted the outcome. For example, subjects whose brain physiology and behaviors were affected by alcohol abuse, as well as individuals who had experienced brain damage, resorted to less adaptive defenses.

Remember that defense mechanisms help us cope, creatively rearranging conflict so we can go about our business without falling apart. In Vaillant's words:

The Inside Holding Pattern

The ego—the integrating principle in our central nervous system—needs to stall for time until mental accommodation can take place. Such alterations in inner and/ or outer reality and emotion must be in lay terms, denied, repressed, or distorted until the accompanying anxiety and depression can be borne. (p. 30)

The ingenuity of the ego in this reality-bending accommodation is illustrated in the following story. Early in one of the studies, a fourteenyear-old told the interviewer that she wanted to be a doctor. Many years later, at age seventyeight, she said in a follow-up interview that she had majored in college in premedical education but had never entertained the possibility of being a physician. Nevertheless, vocational testing conducted when she was thirty indicated that she was interested in both medicine and music. The problem was that her early adulthood in the 1930s had been overshadowed by economic depression, the secondary role of women, and poverty. Stifling her potential, she had immersed herself in a life of necessity. Later circumstances, including a divorce, allowed the resurrection of her disowned passion and activities more in accord with her true spirit. At the age of sixty she began violin lessons and eventually performed in front of a metropolitan audience. We see in this story how initial repression (which lasted for a number of decades) eventually gave way to the flow of creative expression.

The exchange of less mature defenses for more mature ones and the emergence of a new sense of self for the woman just described and other subjects did not happen just by chance. It happened because the brains of the research subjects were growing new neurons and making new connections. Vaillant's data solidly demonstrates that the ego matures through the *internalization of a holding environment*—that is, by holding inside ourselves the image and emotional experience of people we love and who love us. Just as infants take in the soothing mother (as we saw with baby Sarah), we adults can connect to a nurturing source and internally anchor it to become selfsoothers. The experience of being loved, valued, and treasured for who we are then lives within us, filling the aching gaps of isolation and loneliness. In other words, Vaillant is saying it is never too late for attachment! Barring neuronal damage in the developing fetus or injury to brain tissue after birth, to whatever degree we suffered inadequate bonding, opportunity to round out the experience can bring completion *no matter what our age*.

Indeed, the internalization of a holding environment involves the phenomenon of neuroplasticity as new neurons make connections between brain cells. These new connections result from a relationship with someone who takes on a parental, teaching, or emotionally nourishing role. This is why foster parenting and adoption succeed when children are received into loving and psychologically ripe environments. This is why, when we have the good fortune to find mentors who take us under their wings, we internalize an experience of feeling worth the time and energy of someone who treasures us and who may help us resurrect parts of ourselves our parents ignored or even tried to eradicate. This is why relationships steeped in tolerance, patience, and commitment touch hidden pockets of potential we ultimately dare to manifest. This is why it is argued that when God and spiritual deities are taken in as attachment figures, that connection with sources emanating unconditional love opens our hearts.

Robert Johnson (1998), a Jungian analyst, described the mentoring phenomenon beautifully in his autobiographical book, *Balancing Heaven and Earth*. In the chapter interestingly entitled "Finding My True Family," Johnson tells how three people guided and influenced him during his high school years. An only child born to mismatched parents who divorced early in his childhood, Robert felt little parental connection, let alone validation.

While his maternal grandmother, who was in charge of him when his mother worked, offered him some warmth, direction, and a beginning glimpse of the world of music he came to love, there were three other people—a spinster piano teacher named Miss Rand, an organ builder, and an artist—who recognized the potential musician and latent mystic within the recesses of his being and nurtured the evolution of both. Johnson's description of the internalization of a holding environment is classic: "Miss Rand quickly became the mother I always wished that I had been born to, the one person who seemed to understand my Golden World experience and validated my inner world" (p. 25).

One need only read the accounting of the rest of his life—that of the unfolding of his particular kind of genius—to understand the significance of his years of being mentored and what a loss it would have been individually and collectively had these mentors not appeared.

Mentoring is an important experience, because many of us carry talents even the best of parents cannot appreciate. Often it is a teacher or a once-removed relative who recognizes the disempowered spark and fans the flame. Such was the case for Victor. Raised in a brood of six by practical, family-devoted parents, he early on showed interest in art, borrowing books from the library and poring over the works of the masters. His parents were puzzled by what seemed to them an unusual interest for a fourth-grade child, and they could not relate to his enthusiasm. When his uncle from Mexico visited, the situation took a different turn, because not only was the man knowledgeable in art history but he was a painter himself. Together they went to art galleries and museums. Best of all, Victor received his first lesson at the easel of his uncle. His connection to his uncle was one that provided the internal environment for immersion in art and the blossoming of his talent.

Exercise 5.b

- ◊ Do you have an unfulfilled potential that has not been encouraged?
- ◊ What mentoring experiences have influenced you, and in what way?
- ◊ When you feel challenged, do you summon the memory and experience of a mentor's guidance?
- ◊ Have you been a mentor to someone? If so, did it seem to benefit the individual you were mentoring? What did you learn about yourself in the performance of this role? What effect did it have?

Altered States of Consciousness

Do we have a problem here? Do substitute parents, empathic teachers, beneficent tutors, spiritual advisers, compassionate therapists, or in-tune friends and lovers provide the only means for taking in a holding environment? What if no such person comes along?

Fortunately, the threshold of the conscious mind provides another and very natural portal, that of an altered state of consciousness (ASC). ASCs are often equated with terms such as "being in a trance" or "under a hypnotic spell," both of which are misconceptions that only serve to confuse people and block understanding of their benefits. Properly speaking, altered states of consciousness occur when there is a change in how we take in information, how we think, and how we feel. Numerous factors can precipitate ASCs, intoxication or being "strung out" on drugs are familiar examples. Many people do not realize that dreaming at night and the fuzzy states we experience when falling asleep and upon awakening are other examples.

Another way of describing an ASC is *focused attention that we give to something at the exclusion of everything else*. Being totally immersed in a creative project, mesmerized by a novel, or spellbound at a movie are all bona fide experiences of an altered state of consciousness.

This means that moving into an ASC is a natural function of the mind that manifests itself in varying ways and with varying intensities. Depending on their purpose, ASCs can serve us well or they can distract us from reality and even tap into dysfunctional aspects of human nature. Political leaders have been known to sway masses through their charismatic use of words and hypnotic suggestion. Hitler is a classic example of this phenomenon being used for a destructive end. On the other hand, proper use of ASC can activate tremendous healing potential. When Herbert Benson, a physician-researcher at Harvard, wrote his groundbreaking book, *The Relaxation Response* (1975), he revealed the benefits to our bodies and minds from being in a state of relaxation. Whether achieved through meditation, progressive relaxation, yoga, or hypnosis, such focused states counteract the consequences of stress while providing a general quieting of the nervous system. Since Benson's book appeared, we have witnessed an accumulation of a massive amount of evidence regarding the positive effects of the phenomenon Benson described. For example, in the next chapter you will learn scientifically based meditative techniques for dealing with disruptive emotions and thoughts as put forth by psychologist Christopher Germer (2009) in *The Mindful Path to Self-Compassion*.

These adept utilizations of ASCs open the door to healing resources carried deep within each one of us, which are often triggered through the use of imagery during ASC. What we experience as visions, sounds, smells, or touch in our imaginations can have the same physiological effects as if these sensory stimuli were occurring in physical reality. Think of your favorite food when you haven't eaten in a while, and if you are hungry enough, you will start to salivate! That is why more and more books are written about how to mend our bodies with our minds and how to use imagery to evoke healing for our troubled spirits. Andrew Weil (1995), the sage of alternative medicine, emphasizes that the use of imagery during ASC is most beneficial when it is emotion laden. In other words, passion energizes images into healing action. While one patient suffering from a wound infection might imagine a healing potion washing away the offending bacteria with much pleasure, another might imagine shooting each of the little buggers with a BB gun.

Psychotherapists know these principles well, because the use of guided imagery, hypnosis, and active imagination are staples used by many clinicians. And with good reason, for one of the most potent of all is the technique of Eye Movement Desensitization and Reprocessing (EMDR). This technique is a complex process that is individually tailored to the client's needs. The therapist may first ask the client to bring to mind an image of a place that feels safe and calm. While doing so, the client uses her eyes to track the therapist's back-and-forth finger movement. When the positive emotions have increased, the client is asked to repeat the procedure on her own. The client may then be instructed to bring an image of a distressing event to mind while feeling the emotions associated with the image. Once again she uses her eyes to track the therapist's back-and-forth finger movement. This bilateral movement activates processes in the brain that not only facilitate healing of a psychological dynamic frozen in time but also empower the client with the ability to self-soothe.

Mental health practitioners are not alone in describing instances in which individuals meet a teacher, mentor, or spiritual being while in an ASC (Kirkpatrick, 1999). Religious leaders offer countless examples of the faithful taking in the presence of an unconditionally loving figure. New Age thinkers often refer to a realm of goddesses, some of whom befriend and enrich those who seek them. The common denominator is that of an altered state of consciousness in which a narrowed focus at the exclusion of everything else provides an atmosphere of trust. Here, within the bounds of such an experience, our innermost vulnerabilities and potentials can be unconditionally embraced, which stimulates new neuronal growth. And without our conscious knowing, this growth often happens when we are in nature.

Who doesn't know the delights of an open field or wooded area where a flowing creek sings, the gentle wind murmurs, and the trees offer up their soothing protection? Most people would never speak in terms of talking to the "spirit of a tree," yet their inner knowing sits them under a tree where the quiet shifts their focus, lessens their cares, and sometimes produces "light bulb" solutions to their problems. Our connection to nature is primal, and on both conscious and unconscious levels, we are compelled to seek it out even in the way we mount replicas of natural scenes on our walls, gaze at the sky from our office windows, garden in the backyard, hike along wooded trails, watch the Discovery Channel, visit the zoo, or nurture our pets. Connecting with nature is as natural as breathing and eating—it replenishes us.

With nature in mind, it is appropriate to turn our attention to the oldest healing tradition known to humankind: shamanism. Across all cultures and across millennia of time, history shows how human beings have utilized this natural means of connecting with healing sources. No matter what our ethnicity or geographical location, our roots go back to cultures steeped in shamanic tradition. The healing role fell to the tribal shaman, who entered an altered state of consciousness (in shamanic terms, it is referred to as *journeying*) whereby he communicated with other realms to obtain power and information to heal those entrusted to his care.

The mission of shamanic journeying is that of betterment of the human condition through natural and spiritual means, and its traditions have much to offer us as we strive for ego growth. Religious historian Mircea Eliade (1964) describes the holistic nature of the shaman as he treats mind and body, heart and soul through sacred connection—connection that relies on the natural facility of the mind to communicate with sources of information beyond the finite self.

Journeying has not only been a shamanic staple over the centuries. Thanks to Michael Harner (1980) and The Foundation for Shamanic Studies, it is now flourishing in this time of tremendous need. Journeying is a technique that can be learned by anyone, and each year Harner's organization teaches journeying to thousands of individuals around the world in weekend trainings. No longer a modality used just by a formal shaman, journeying allows any of us to move into an altered state of consciousness to tap inner resources and apply healing knowledge to ourselves. Self-empowering in this way, journeying resonates with the notion of individual responsibility as well as personal participation in the healing process.

Is there a relationship between shamanism and science? Generally, studies investigating the effects of ASCs have produced positive healing results.

Specifically, research conducted by psychologist and shamanic practitioner Sandra Harner (1995) measured the effect of shamanic drumming and journeying on immune response and emotional affect. While there was no significant impact on immune response, a distinct response regarding emotional states was reported, including reductions in anxiety, anger, confusion, depression, and fatigue. In addition, The Foundation for Shamanic Studies engages in numerous ongoing research endeavors that demonstrate and advance the healing efficacy of shamanic altered states of consciousness.

How does this look from the standpoint of growing up the ego? Jung (1967) was dipping into shamanic territory himself when he described how nature provides countless mothering archetypes that nourish and soothe us, including animals, real or not. This is what occurs in shamanic journeying when journeyers enter an ASC and encounter animal helpers. In my book, *Journeying: Where Shamanism and Psychology Meet* (1998), I relate a number of such journeys wherein power animals and spirit guides offer a lifelong connection of inner alliance, safety, protection, and nurturing—in other words, the internalization of a holding environment.

This internalization of a holding environment is illustrated in the first journey of Ted, a thirtyeight-year-old convenience store manager who was mourning the end of his marriage of twelve years. Ted had done considerable reading about divorce and made a conscious decision not to date until he brought closure to his grieving. He also had a passing acquaintance with the notion of power animals and wanted to see if this approach would bring him solace and internal connection. After being given journeying instructions and settling into a recliner with earphones feeding him the sound of a beating drum, this (in abbreviated form) is what Ted described as he spoke his journey aloud:

> *I hear the drum and I find myself next to a familiar lake. I take a deep breath and look around for an opening in the ground. I remember where there is a boggy place on the north side and walk over there and step into the squish. I feel myself going down—amazing how this works—I'm okay.*
>
> *Here I am slipping and sliding down through an opening in the mud. I see a light at the end of this tunnel and now I am coming out into a field. I still hear the drum. I know I'm here to look for my power animal, but all I see is grass and a clump of trees over to the side. I think I'll walk over there. Gee, when I get to the trees all of a sudden I'm in a jungle! I can feel the moisture and the heat and I can hear the call of a strange bird. I feel like I should be careful but I'm really not afraid. I hope I find my power animal.*
>
> *I see a monkey swinging from a tree but it's not paying any attention to me. Oh— there's a lion standing off to my right about ten yards ahead. It almost takes my breath away. It's standing very still. I can't seem to say it out loud, but in my mind I ask, "Are you my power animal?" It looks directly at me and I know it is. Then it's standing right next to me and I feel a shiver.*
>
> *Something makes my hand reach out to touch its fur. And now I'm riding on its back—fast across the ground—I've never felt like this before. We stop at a river and sit next to each other. I become aware*

> *of the lion's heart beating like the drum and remember the cowardly lion in* The Wizard of Oz *who wanted a heart for courage.*
>
> *But this is love—I feel it coming from the lion's heart. (Tears are streaming down his face.) I feel safe and comforted—somehow I know I'm going to get through all this pain. I hear the drum beating faster and know I'm supposed to end the journey. The lion lets me know she will wait for me to come again. I wave goodbye and I'm coming back out the way I got here.*

When Ted said that he knew he would get through all of this, it signaled an encouraging shift in his condition, because up to the point at which he sought help, he had flirted with the idea of suicide. The divorce had opened unresolved wounds from his childhood, a time when he had been abandoned by a single mother and left in the care of an aunt who was chronically ill and too weak to give him the attention he needed. As Ted immersed himself in journeying experiences, the lion, a steadfast protector and guide, soothed his spirit and inspired hope for a better future. Here we have a powerful example of the internalization of a holding environment through the use of journeying and alliance with a shamanic power animal that provided the kind of nurturing Ted had not experienced in his formative years.

Not everyone "journeys" in such a traditional way. Years of experience have taught me that some individuals have unique ways of interacting with a power animal without even being acquainted with shamanism. One woman, an avid hiker, encountered a bear on four separate occasions in the wilderness, and she decided to begin meeting with "the bear"—always taking the same route (up the trail to a favorite tree)—in her imagination. What ensued was a full-blown mentoring experience. As she relaxed on her day bed and slipped into a reverie, she and the bear engaged in their own kind of dialogue. Sometimes the bear threw things at her, objects she would hold in her hands and talk about while the bear sat on his haunches and listened. She found herself sometimes crying but also laughing, as her stories poured forth. She realized after several months of this that she had recounted most of her life's story to the bear, even secrets she had revealed to no one. The bear, with the soft gaze of his steady eyes, gave her a presence she had never experienced. She found a new strength rising within herself, and put it this way: "Getting all that stuff out of me freed me up. I don't care so much anymore what others think of me. Every time I visit the bear, I come away feeling I've touched something new inside me that gives me power I didn't have before. The bear is my friend for life."

In one final example, Beth, a former client who had been physically and sexually abused in her childhood, experienced her wounded child outside herself. Through a long series of journeys during which she imagined the little girl sitting alone on a log, she, the adult Beth, with the aid of her power animal, slowly began to approach the child. The child at first would not allow herself to be touched and would only scream out her pain as the power animal and adult Beth held her energetically in loving acceptance. During succeeding journeys, the outbursts gradually gave way to calm and cautious watching. Eventually, she let herself be touched and even held physically by Beth until, in the end, the adult and the child merged.

Emotion-laden imagery, as mentioned previously, carries the greatest likelihood for healing activity both in physical and psychological realms. Sometimes emotion coupled with imagery surprises us, because we lack an awareness that such feelings even exist within. In the foregoing examples, without such linking of imagery to emotion, healing activity would not have occurred.

Connecting with nature, encountering helpful figures (whether imagined or real), and experiencing calming and soothing acceptance is available to anyone who carries both healing intent and staying power for the ongoing venture. Some of us do this naturally and spontaneously. Some of us need the direction of a person trained in ASC. Once learned, ASC can be a helpful tool for the rest of our lives.

Learning how to self-soothe is essential in growing up the ego. Whether by means of mentoring, journeying, active imagination, a therapeutic relationship, or any other manner, anchoring this ability through taking nurturing figures inside is alchemical. In other words, experiences of loneliness and angst are transformed into loving connections both within ourselves and with others. Neurologically, new neural linkages of being loved unconditionally develop in the brain, and like straw spun into gold, ego-growing-up work spins the rough and the raw into the fine and the mature.

Exercise 5.c

Are internalized figures of loved ones incorporated into your capacity to self-nurture? ◊ How often do you use such figures in times of stress?

Exercise 5.d

In the coming week, notice any onset of emotional distress and see if you can apply a comforting memory or image that calms you. Examples include imagining a calm natural setting, being with someone you love, listening to music, going for a walk, meditating, or whatever appeals to you.

In addition to journaling your results, share your responses with your support person and also share how you plan to continue honing this self-nurturing capacity.

In Closing

Our psychological defenses can and do mature. This maturing process results from the ongoing resolution of our spiral issues and the honing of our capacity to self-nurture. Then, no matter our age or our situation, we find our rhythm increasingly synchronized to self-loving—the only spring from which loving others can flow.

In this chapter, you have learned about the spiral of growth and how your life issues intersect this spiral in ongoing ways. Vaillant's research illustrated how it is never too late to grow up your ego and how the internalizing of a nurturing environment is integral to emotional growth. You read examples of how the use of altered states of consciousness can anchor such a holding environment and were reminded of the pivotal role nature offers in helping you hold yourself secure.

In the next chapter, you will discover what scientists have to say about emotions, how emotions impact the mind-body connection, how vital emotions are to healthy living, and how to counteract feeling emotionally overwhelmed by creating an inner environment in which new connections in the brain can be made.

WORKS CITED

Benson, H. (1975). *The relaxation response.* New York: Avon.

Eliade, M. (1964). *Shamanism: Archaic techniques of ecstasy.* Bollingen Series LXXVI, (W. R. Trask, Trans.). Princeton, NJ: Princeton University Press.

Gagan, J. M. (1998). *Journeying: Where shamanism and psychology meet.* Santa Fe, NM: Rio Chama Publications.

Germer, C. K. (2009). *The mindful path to selfcompassion: Freeing yourself from destructive thoughts and emotions.* New York: Guilford Press.

Harner, M. (1980). *The way of the shaman: A guide to power and healing.* San Francisco: Harper & Row.

Harner, S. D. (1995). *Immune and affect response to shamanic drumming.* (Doctoral dissertation, Fordham University ETD Collection, January 1, 1995.) Retrieved from http://fordham.bepress.com/dissertations/AAI9520609

Johnson, R. A. (1998). *Balancing heaven and earth.* San Francisco: Harper.

Jung, C. J. (1967). Symbols of transformation (2nd ed.). In *The Collected Works.* Vol. 5. Bollingen Series XX, (R. F. C. Hull, Trans.). Princeton, NJ: Princeton University Press.

Kirkpatrick, L. A. (1999). Attachment and religious representations and behavior. In J. Cassidy & P. R. Shaver (Eds.), *Handbook of attachment: Theory, research, and clinical applications* (pp. 803-822). New York: Guilford Press.

Vaillant, G. E. (1993). *The wisdom of the ego.* Cambridge, MA: Harvard University Press. Weil, A. (1995). *Spontaneous healing.* New York: Knopf.

EMOTIONS ON THE MOVE

The flow of water, with its variable pace and force, provides a compelling image for emotions. The very word emotion means "to set into motion" or "move the feelings." And now that your spiral issues are enumerated and your ability to self-nurture activated, it is time to hone your emotional perspective. In this chapter, you will learn the true nature of emotion, what it means to be in proper relationship to its flow, and how the right use of emotions accelerates growth. The chapter questions and exercises will guide you to a deeper understanding of your own emotions as well as ways in which to appropriately regulate them.

Overview

Again we touch base with what was learned in chapter 2 regarding the impact of caregivers' actions and reactions to the infant's emotional states. Through this current of interchanges, the infant's immature psychology is shaped by the parent's more mature psychology, with resulting behavioral patterns that range from healthy to dysfunctional—for most of us, a mixture of each.

From the beginning to the end of our lives, emotions are central to how we experience ourselves and are pivotal in maturing our defenses and growing up our egos. As we saw in chapter 3, the sixth stage of self-awareness challenges us to become more in touch with the complexity of our perceptions, sensations, and feelings. Without doubt, cultivating the relationship we have to our feeling states is partner to that big shift half way up the growth spiral. This comes about in a variety of ways. For some, knowing the difference between thoughts and feelings is the first step. For others, appreciating the value of emotions is the task at hand. And for all, learning how to maneuver in the face of difficult feeling states can make the difference between an empowered and meaningful existence and lives continually plagued by turmoil.

Ideally, our emotions flow through us as nimbly as the river winding round the bend, but individually we are all quite adept at building dams. For as we remember from chapter 4, defense mechanisms serve their function by protecting us from emotions too overwhelming to handle. The many emotions that swirl through us—sometimes within the short span of minutes—can be very confusing and apt to impact how we live each day in negative ways.

Psychotherapists engage in countless explanations debunking myths about our feeling states. The problem is that too often we were taught about the "good" ones and the "bad" ones, learning to deny and hide the likes of sadness, anger, disappointment, and frustration while "putting on a happy face." How regularly we shy away from strong emotions, our own as well as others, reflects this basic predicament. Reinforced by suggestions from religious sources, we may carry a mental list of ways our emotions keep us from being holy or holistic, and for some, an X is placed next to feelings thought to be sinful. Few have learned the critical difference between feeling an emotion and acting it out in harmful ways. We are rightly horrified by wanton acts of violence and destruction. At the same time, we don't know what to do when our own rumblings of discontent get us into trouble due to spiteful words we've spewed forth or hurtful actions we've devised.

Before exploring the true nature of emotions and how to wholesomely deal with them, distinction is made between emotion (feelings) and thought. The world of thought is made up of definitions, ideas, principles, facts, and concepts that reside in our thinking brain. Emotions are biologically rooted impulses toward movement and action that spring from a more rudimentary part of our brain, as well as registering throughout our entire body. Confusion about these two distinct functions often occurs because feelings— such as sadness, fear, joy, and love—are the subjective experiences of emotion and are best expressed in terms of "I feel angry," "I am frustrated," etc. On the other hand, thoughts involve objective beliefs and facts and are expressed in terms of "I believe," "I know," etc. You will find as you read on that the words *emotion* and *feeling* (including *feeling state*) are acceptably used interchangeably.

Science And Emotions

Charles Darwin (1872) was among the first to study emotions, reasoning that emotions are key to the survival of the fittest. In his observations of how we humans share common facial expressions of fear, anger, disgust, enjoyment, and sadness, his results correctly concluded that the emotions of fear and anger are inextricably woven into the fight-or-flight responses (and our survival).

When reptiles and lizards were the highest forms of life on the earth, their brains (a type referred to as "lizard brain") took care of body maintenance and survival functions such as respiration, circulation, and metabolism. As mammals emerged, the "leopard midbrain" (now called the limbic system) expanded out of the lizard brain with the capacity for emotions and coordination of movement. (Here is where the fight-or-flight response waits in readiness.) Over time, the learning frontal brain, or cerebral cortex, evolved, which carries on all human thinking functions and allows us to use language and numbers, to remember things, and to link cause and effect so that we can solve problems.

Until recently, it was believed that the seat of emotions rested solely in the limbic system of the brain, the part that in emergencies springs immediately into action without consulting the rational part of the brain. In less dire instances, messages are sent from the limbic system to the frontal brain through circuits involving a network of neurons, synapses, and neurotransmitters. Neurons, or nerve cells, communicate with each other through informational impulses and chemical substances called neurotransmitters that help these impulses cross the gap (or synapse) between them. When this system is in good working order, information gets to where it needs to go in the frontal brain, allowing us to perceive clearly what is happening, to integrate the experience of it, and then to choose an appropriate direction of behavior.

In addition to this brain circuitry, researchers are now informing us of another system of emotional flow. Within this system, informationbearing chemicals called neuropeptides are distributed like a web throughout the entire body— uniting mind and body and diminishing the notion of the mind-body split.

Using the blood and cerebrospinal fluid as their medium of travel, neuropeptides lock into cell receptors and are involved in the regulation of body functioning and feeling states while the same information is registering in our brains.

Researcher Candace Pert (1997) initiated this avenue of scientific pursuit when she used morphine to ferret out the opiate receptor, discovering that when morphine locks into the opiate receptor in the cell, the good feelings begin. Made either by the body (endorphins) or taken in from the outside (drugs such as morphine), these substances do indeed produce pleasurable feelings. Blood endorphins in hamsters increase close to 200 percent from the beginning to the end of the sex act! Furthermore, "runner's high" is no exaggeration. Such examples of endorphin production inside our bodies are too often overshadowed by the pursuit of substances we can swallow or inject to activate our pleasure receptors.

The endorphin neuropeptide is only one of the substances affecting our emotions. Anxiety receptors bind with anxiety-structured neuropeptides, excitement receptors bind with excitement-structured neuropeptides, and so on. Mood-altering neuropeptides are found in our brains *and* in our blood, bones, muscles, and organs—the heart itself is home to every neuropeptide receptor. High concentrations of neuropeptide receptors strung along the spinal cord and situated around our five senses are viewed as nodal points or "hot spots" where large volumes of information come together. With the stimulation of a sense organ such as the skin, emotions may be immediately triggered because, in addition to memories being stored in the mind, the body holds memories as well. Cell receptors in the skin responding to touch do so colored by memories of previous touching. Our past emotional experiences affect how information flows, how we move and hold our bodies, causing Pert (1997) to conclude in her book, *Molecules of Emotion*:

> Emotions and body sensations are thus intricately intertwined in a bi- directional network in which each can alter the other. Usually this process takes place at an unconscious level, but it can also surface into consciousness under certain conditions or be brought into consciousness by intention (p. 142).

So we see that the electrical neurotransmitter system and the chemical neuropeptide system together engage in a constant flow of information exchange that not only orchestrates our moods and engineers our behaviors but also is fundamentally involved in total body physiology. Consequently, neuroscience, endocrinology, and immunology are linked in this sea of peptide communication afloat with emotions that connect brain, body, and behavior. As we learned in the previous chapter, the term *neuroplasticity* refers to the brain's flexibility in creating new connections by growing new nerve endings. Such discoveries—the capacity of the brain to produce new cells even in conditions of aging and injury—have scientists thinking in revolutionary ways about healing. At the same time we, the people, are reforming our notions about physical and mental health and the curative measures we pursue. Increasingly, alternative approaches to healing (which view the body as a mirror of the mind) are being turned to, with mainstream medicine keeping an eye out for if and where they fit in.

How we think about our feeling experiences and relate to them is crucial to the proper functioning of this mind-body connection. Being accurately informed about the nature and purpose of emotions shapes the foundation of this understanding, and Pert (1997) minces no words in delivering her perspective:

> *All* emotions are healthy because emotions are what unite the mind and body. Anger, fear, and sadness, the so-called negative emotions, are as healthy as peace, courage, and joy. To repress these emotions and not let them flow freely is to set up a dis-integrity in the system, causing it to act at cross purposes, rather than a unified whole. The stress this creates, to maintain function at the cellular level, is what sets up the weakened conditions that can lead to disease. All honest emotions are positive emotions (pp. 192-193).

Exercise 6.a

Which emotions are easiest for you to feel and accept? (See Feeling Word List, Appendix B.)

Exercise 6.b

Write down the emotion that is most difficult for you to feel and accept. In your journal, begin making daily notations of:

1. when you notice the feeling within yourself and how you handle it: through expression, by pushing it aside, by allowing it to be what it is, by judging it, etc.; and
2. when you notice this identified feeling being expressed by another, jot down how you react to it: with fear, judgment, dismissal, acknowledgment, etc.

Emotions Are Smart

Emotions are smart because they carry information that makes the difference between life and death. Molecules of emotion register fear in the body, alerting us to danger and energizing us to run at breakneck speeds. Molecules of emotion trigger anger when we are assaulted and mobilize hormones for amazing acts of defense and heroism.

Emotions are smart because they carry information that connects us with reality. Molecules of emotion register sadness when we lose someone close to us, opening up healing torrents of grief. Molecules of emotion register guilt when we fail to live up to a commitment, prompting an upgrade of conduct or reassessment of the obligation.

Emotions are smart because they carry information that connects us to others, thereby improving our quality of life. Molecules of emotion record happiness when we are rightly rewarded for our efforts, stirring us to share our good fortune in celebratory ways. Molecules of emotion resonate with love when our child spontaneously hugs us, melting away the day's collection of frayed nerves and irritated responses.

Conscious Awareness Of Emotions

Appreciating the basic integrity of emotion is a huge step. The correct use of emotion is an even bigger one and calls for the midbrain and the forebrain to communicate with each other on an ongoing basis. As we know, the emotional part of the brain was in place long before the thinking brain. The neural circuitry that eventually evolved between the two is an indispensable loop that, when in good working order, allows for messages to be sent back and forth between the two. Because the amygdala (a structure in the limbic midbrain) remembers the emotional flavor of events, it offers emotional intelligence to the frontal cortex. Thus, when we need to make a decision, it is important for the front brain to huddle with the midbrain. For example, if I decide to move to another part of the country and am uncertain as to which environment would suit me best, I need to revisit emotional memories of being in a locale where it rains all the time, of living in the country, of being surrounded by high-rises in the city, and so on. This involves *bringing heart to head*.

Just as important is *bringing head to heart*, whereby thinking intelligence is brought to emotional states. This dynamic is exemplified by Bernie, a Vietnam War veteran suffering from post-traumatic stress disorder (PTSD). At the first sign of recurring anxiety, Bernie remembers to connect with his front brain, to utilize the stressreducing exercises he has learned, thereby chipping away at his rising level of distress. Similarly, when little Andy stops to remember that if he hits Todd again he'll be sent to the corner, he is using his thoughts to moderate his feelings.

Bringing head to heart and heart to head involve different types of intelligence. Daniel Goleman (1995), author of *Emotional Intelligence*, tells us that standard IQ tests measure a type of academic intelligence that has next to no relationship to emotional intelligence. Emotional intelligence carries "a key set of other characteristics" that contribute to the quality of life we all long for: ". . . abilities such as being able to motivate oneself and persist in the face of frustrations; to control impulse and delay gratification; to regulate one's moods and keep distress from swamping the ability to think; to empathize and to hope" (p. 34).

Notice how these words resonate with descriptions of the mature defense mechanisms, particularly sublimation, suppression, anticipation, and altruism in chapter 4. Furthermore, Goleman explains that when the static of strong emotions muddies the circuit between the limbic system and the frontal cortex, it sabotages the ability of the prefrontal lobe to maintain memory and creates deficits in our intellectual capacities. Neuroscientist and psychiatrist Daniel Amen (1998) further emphasizes this mental health predicament in his outline of specific conditions resulting from limbic systems driven by unchecked emotion. This list includes moodiness, irritability, depression, negative thinking, negative perception of events, decreased motivation, appetite and sleep problems, obsessiveness, impulsiveness, decreased or overactive sexual responsiveness, bonding disruptions, and premenstrual syndrome.

Fortunately, the downside of this situation is offset by the neuroplasticity of the brain. Brain imaging techniques show how ingrained behaviors and attitudes are replaced by healthier and more nourishing ones. As researcher Joe Dispenza (2007) so brilliantly details in his book, *Evolve Your Brain*, the frontal lobe is wired to learn new things. Very specifically, astrocyte cells, which make up nearly half the brain's cells, not only enhance the speed of neurological transmission but also help to form synaptic connections. To consciously activate new firings across the gap between associated neurons involves commitment and focus—exactly what the exercises in this book promote. For example, the stronger the focus on replacing self-criticizing thoughts with the belief and images of being loved, the stronger the signal sent across the synapses between neurons. The more intense the experiences of self-nurturing, the more potent the messages sent to the neighboring nerve cells. Mental rehearsal and repetition are essential in the creation of these new linkages for, as brain researchers say: "neurons that fire together, wire together" (quote attributed to neuropsychologist Donald Hebb).

While Pert studies cellular emotion, Goleman focuses on emotional intelligence, and Amen and Dispenza map out how to change the brain's reactions, the core of overlap in each of their messages boils down to this:

- ◊ Emotions supply information essential for healthy living.
- ◊ Awareness of our emotions is crucial for their effective utilization.
- ◊ The frontal cortex of the brain is key in changing neural synapses that help us to regulate our emotions.

An Emotional Intersection

Growth requires bringing forth our emotions, yet we also know that our defense mechanisms keep threatening emotions at bay. How do we proceed through this intersection of seemingly oppositional dynamics? As we have seen, by calling on your frontal cortex, you can initiate efforts to grow into the more mature defense mechanisms of suppression, anticipation, sublimation, humor, and altruism. Such an investment will not only help you advance, it will also stretch your emotional resilience and strengthen your base of resources.

The dynamic of the mature defense of suppression provides a valuable example, as it involves bringing awareness to a feeling (such as anger) and using the forebrain to negotiate if, how, and when to deal with the energy of this state. Recall the tale from chapter 4 of the divorcing mother who chose to suppress her rage throughout the court proceedings and to ventilate with appropriate safeguards in place—in the presence of her support system.

Sublimation, another mature defense, involves the choice to channel emotional energy into safe outlets. For example, a friend of mine was extremely upset when she developed a stress fracture in her foot that brought a halt to her lunchtime walks and weekend hikes. Never before curtailed in physical activity, she knew she had the choice of stewing in her juices (which she knew would compound the degree of emotional fallout) or finding a way to sublimate the energy. In spite of limited swimming ability and distaste for chlorine swimming pools, she listened to the doctor's suggestion and dove in. Now she's quick to convey how many laps she swims, glad for the addition to her athletic skills, and pleased with the advancement in the capacity to empower herself. In other words, the brain changed as new patterns produced growth of new connections between cells.

As we saw previously, the ego-growth stages show us the intersection between expanded and psychological growth. Specifically, the call to selfawareness sounded by the sixth stage signals the beginning of a shift from external blame to internal self-responsibility as we take on captainship of how we emotionally express ourselves. Remember the road sign in chapter 3 used to indicate the juncture between the self-aware and conscientious stages: "Caution: self-reflection, reconstruction, and more responsibility ahead." During this passage we cross the gulf between "You make me feel this way" (blaming others) to "When X happens, I feel Y" (taking responsibility).

This awareness can spring from a number of different sources. We may notice that not everyone has the same response to external events or that a situation that causes me anger on one day does not on the next. When greeted at work by a supervisor demanding the impossible, I may puzzle when my work partner is not as disturbed as I am. Or, if he is, I may be struck by his way of going about solving the situation. As a result of attempts at better communication and listening to a family member in a less judgmental way, I may be stunned to discover her internal feeling map differs from mine.

Waking up to individual feeling and thinking differences contributes to understanding that responsibility for *my unique response* to situations and people in my life resides in *me*—part and parcel of the work of ego-growth stages six, seven, and eight and the growth of new neurons.

Exercise 6.c

Recall a time when you were in a difficult situation (physical limitation, rageful feelings toward a family member or friend, frustration with a coworker, etc.) and you chose to employ a mature defense mechanism instead of responding in a conflicting or distressing way. Record this situation in your journal and put a smile after it, as a reminder of your capacity to transform detrimental behaviors and attitudes into mature ones.

Emotional Hijacking

But what about times when the connection between the amygdala and the frontal cortex is tangled or not operating at all? What about times when, objectively speaking, no emotional emergency exists and we act as if one does? What about those who seem to be in a perpetual state of emergency? Goleman (1995) refers to such instances as "emotional hijacking," the limbic system's amygdala reacting to a situation such as an emergency when none exists. The reason is this: when emotional emergencies actually happen, arousal of the amygdala stamps the memory with an emotional imprint of the event (the stronger the arousal, the stronger the imprint). The amygdala continues to compare present happenings to happenings of the past, and "when one key element of a present situation is similar to the past, the amygdala can call it a 'match' and act before there is full confirmation" (p. 21).

Given the distribution of molecules of emotion throughout the body, "one key element" might be touch to a part of the body previously abused or glimpse of a facial expression akin to Dad's before his belt delivered his blow. During Sue Ann's childhood, her grandfather, a man who had a beard, sexually abused her. It wasn't until she was in her mid-thirties and exploring seemingly unprovoked emotional emergencies that she realized initial attractions to bearded men quickly degenerated into hysterical reactions and irrational accusations. Similarly, Paul's mother, a very distracted woman who spent most of her time on the telephone with friends, time and time again brushed his childhood bids for attention aside. Later when his wife or fellow workers did not listen to him with undivided attention, Paul flew into unreasonable rages.

Whether from the imprint of one intense emotional violation or the accumulation of emotional wounds from childhood, the amygdala resonates to similarities in the present and acts accordingly. When such emotional emergencies repeatedly respond to false alarms while bypassing the ability to reason, the fallout leaves the individual with even more internal distress, contributing to demoralized relationships and jeopardized livelihoods.

Furthermore, the constant outpouring of stress hormones in the body compromises the immune system and endangers physical health—resulting in many of the conditions that appear on Daniel Amen's previously noted list (see p. 78).

While many individuals do not have extreme emotional blueprints imperiling them, to varying and lesser degrees we all carry history of limbic imprinting that, under specific circumstances, leaves us vulnerable to emotional hijacking. Dawn is a good example. A successful entrepreneur who managed most of her business by telephone and online promotions, she was petrified of having to speak in public—a likely, but dreaded next step in the expansion of her business. The rest of Dawn's mental health profile was healthy, including a satisfying marriage with two seemingly well-adjusted children, close friends, and a balance of work and play. Nonetheless, any suggestion of public speaking terrified her, including a guest attendance at a Toastmasters' meeting where she sat paralyzed from beginning to end. Dawn was emotionally hijacked.

Exploring the genesis of this situation, she described how, in the fifth grade, while giving reports in front of the class, her teacher repeatedly commented on her halting, quavering voice and insisted she speak more from her diaphragm. Her peers took up the criticism and dubbed her "quacky." Obviously, more than once in Dawn's early years, amygdala arousal around public speaking reached a fever pitch. Now her alert system was still waiting for the crowd to shout out "quacky." Dawn's faulty circuitry was eventually corrected through application of the technique Eye Movement Desensitization and Reprocessing (described on page 67), allowing her to speak effectively before audiences in a resonant and clear voice.

On the other hand, Jason's life was rendered inept by emotional hijacking. At age 28, he was jobless, homeless, and without support of family or friends. The local mental health center that Jason sometimes frequented described this man as out of control and unable to take directions of any kind. Having grown up in a home with substance-abusing parents, Jason's history of adequate bonding was very weak. By the time he was in middle school, he was out on the street fending for himself, becoming well known for his impulsive nature and quick temper. The slightest hint of putdown or the curious glance of a stranger could set off a rage. Jason's raw and wounded limbic system left him defenseless, the cognitive portion of his brain unavailable as a resource for emotional regulation. Unfortunately, he was unable to follow through with the needed help offered by the mental health center because of his inability to keep appointments.

Obviously, the circuitry between the limbic system and the front brain needs to be as open as the pathways traveled by the molecules of emotion throughout our bodies. Acknowledging and relating to our emotions is the next step.

Exercise 6.d

Record in your journal several examples in your life when you experienced being emotionally hijacked—times when your reaction seemed unwarranted by the situation. Is there a common underlying emotional cause to them, such as fear, anger, sadness, or other feeling states? As you identify underlying causes, write down the consequences of these hijacked emotions not being recognized, felt, and expressed in a healthy way. Place a star µ next to this journal entry as this information is relevant to further exercises in this chapter.

Say Hello to Your Emotions

In my early years, I imitated my parents and siblings by not saying what I was feeling. One day in my bedroom while ironing a school dress, my stepmother happened by the open door. Startled, I quickly ran to hide the picture of my hoped-for beau, temporarily perched in full view. Of course, she saw it, but we did not speak of the moment. In fact, I wouldn't have known how to say I felt embarrassed, so accustomed was I to brushing aside such occurrences and pretending they didn't exist. We proceeded as if nothing had happened. As trivial as this event may seem, it later helped me realize how out of touch I was with my childhood and adolescent feeling states.

So what does it mean to bring emotions into awareness intentionally? Is thinking about what I feel enough? Should I be telling everyone what I feel all the time? What do I do if I'm not aware of my feelings much of the time?

Though all of us carry at least some awareness of feelings, a distinction often is made between "thinking" and "feeling" types. Feelers are described as more tender minded, making decisions based on subjective values, and reacting more emotionally to events. The more toughminded thinkers seek order through impersonal logic, their emotions superseded by the need to reason out whatever situation is at hand. Jed bursts into tears when told the family dog has been hit by a car, while his brother Tom asks if the vet has been called. The often-heard account of husband John wanting to figure out what to do about a problem while wife Mary wails that he never listens to her feelings is another prototype of the feeling-thinking dichotomy. The short of it is that those who predominately operate from a thinking place have yet to learn to stretch more into feeling awareness and expansion (bringing heart to head), while the feelers have much to learn about bringing reflection and insight to their emotions (bringing head to heart).

Goleman (1995) refers to the work of psychologist John Mayer, whose research reveals three distinctive styles in which people are aware of and deal with their emotions:

1. Self-aware: These individuals are not only aware of their feeling states, they have good personal boundaries and tend to have a positive outlook. Figuring out ways to adjust their feelings, their selfawareness enables them to be in charge of their emotions.
2. Engulfed: These are the people who feel overwhelmed by their emotions even though they are not very consciously aware of them. Swept by ever- changing feeling tides, they have no perspective on how to take charge of them and may appear out of control, obviously falling prey to emotional hijacking.
3. Accepting: This type includes those who are accepting of their moods and (a) are usually in good moods so do little to change them, or (b) are prone to bad moods and also do little to change them (as seen in depressed people who resign themselves to anguish, a paralyzed form of emotional hijacking).

Exercise 6.e

Whether thinker or feeler, self-aware, accepting, or engulfed, none of us escapes the effects of emotion. Think of a time in childhood when your feelings (irrespective of behavior) were frowned upon by the big folks. Now think about a recent time when you argued with your feelings, telling yourself that there is no reason "for feeling that way." Can you see a connection between these two incidents?

Saying hello to our emotions—acquiring more awareness about the validity of all their varieties— means we connect with them in order to receive the information they have to offer. This moving into awareness involves replacing resistance with curiosity, judgment with focus, and fear with trust as we allow emotions to speak their truths, all the while fostering their connections with the forebrain where opportunity for appropriate guidance resides. When brain researcher Joseph LeDoux (1996) says, ". . . emotions are things that happen to us rather than things we will to occur" (p. 19), he reinforces our appreciation of feelings being a part of living—as natural as breathing, eating, and sleeping.

Furthermore, in explaining how *conscious feelings* are no different than other things that hold our mind's attention, LeDoux states, "There is but one mechanism of consciousness, and it can be occupied by mundane facts or highly charged emotions" (p. 19). What is suggested here is that, just as we are aware of the shape, size, and color of a concrete object such as a table, we can identify an emotion that grips us and develop an observer's stance toward its characteristics. Take the example of anxiety: what is its feel (like needles, a prickly ball, a shaky slope)? Where in the body do I feel it (chest, stomach, spine, throat)? What is its shape (triangular, square, round, oblong)? What does it feel like it is made of (foam, concrete, rubber, glass)? Describing in words, drawing on paper, singing out a song, all facilitate connection with the feeling. Just as when we say hello to a friend and begin a conversation, saying hello to a feeling begins a movement toward better understanding of its nature and digesting the fruit of its knowledge.

Exercise 6.f

Some individuals know when they are mad, sad, glad, or scared, yet still have difficulty identifying more subtle feeling states. In these instances, implementing a "Feelings Log" is a valuable way to wake up to the great nuance of emotion and the role it plays in daily lives. (See Appendix B for a Feeling Word List.)

Each day for a week, designate three times when you will stop what you're doing so you can write down what you are feeling in that moment. Start the note with "Hello," and then greet the emotion, such as: "Hello, anxiety" or "Hello, sadness."

Exercise 6.g

Write the label "Emotional Regulation" on a new journal page. Then write a description of how you plan to handle the most difficult feeling you identified in Exercise 6.b. Examples include:

- ◊ "I will acknowledge the presence of this feeling. I will rate its intensity from 1 to 10" (10 being the highest).
- ◊ "I will review the ways in which I've handled or not handled this emotion in the past and come up with new ideas for how to connect the awareness of it with my front brain."
- ◊ "I will list these ideas—such as taking a deep breath; taking a time-out; switching my focus to a self-nurturing image; writing to or talking with my support person, etc."
- ◊ "I will experiment with the ideas I've listed and will rate the intensity of the emotion and the effectiveness of my intervention."

Let's take a look at Kevin as a model for this exercise. He sights a friend across the grocery aisle engrossed in conversation. Not having seen this friend since an incident in which Kevin felt wronged in a major way, a flood of feelings—primarily anger—usurps his relaxed state of mind so much so that he wants to yell out the truth or flatten the guy with a punch in the nose. Since Kevin has been focusing on paying attention to his feeling states, a thought flickers by: "I'm really angry, and this anger is so red-hot it wants to hit." Fast-forwarding to the next step of relating to his emotion, Kevin wonders: "What might my front brain say about this?" Creeping around to another aisle, he takes a time-out while pretending to read the ingredients on a Rice Krispies box. Kevin realizes this is not the time and place to deal with this dilemma. He quietly finishes his grocery shopping and goes home to deepen the connection between his anger and the cells in his frontal cortex.

We will check back in with Kevin later, but for now this example shows how Kevin, in allowing full awareness of his feeling of anger, did not tell himself he shouldn't feel that way nor did he blindly act it out. He honored anger's truth and made strides to say hello to his emotion. A further bonus to using this ability is that we begin to hear others in a different way. When friends or family confide their feeling states, we can imagine the river of emotion moving or wanting to move inside them, knowing that spoken judgment interrupts their flow. More often than not, feelings that are spoken and accepted for what they are facilitate removal of static from brain circuitry, making room for clearer thinking, focused problem solving, and of course, healthier neuroplasticity connections.

At the same time, whether hearing others or ourselves being emotionally expressive, we have the opportunity to notice: What feelings am I aware of here? Which ones seem foreign to me? Which ones do I avoid? Which ones do I seek out? Which ones do I talk about? Which ones do I hide?

Responding as honestly as possible to these six questions, even privately, crosses a threshold in the right use of emotions.

Exercise 6.h

Copy these six questions into your journal. Think of a recent instance when someone was sharing their emotions with you. Now answer the six questions in relation to this example.

Right Use Of Emotions

Herein lies true emotional treasure, for when a feeling state free of hijacking emergencies connects to the frontal cortex, it has the opportunity for *right use*—the act of awareness having brought it to this place. Wendy can yell at her boss or take some deep breaths, using some moments to decide if she can speak with calm and reason or wait until she has had time to connect cognitively. Oscar can realize his sadness and anger when a relationship ends and call a friend (perhaps a number of them) who will listen to his outpouring while the runway to the cognitive part of his brain slowly lights up with information (yes, there had been signs this wouldn't last; no, this person wasn't the best match in the world) that contributes to the integration of the experience. Lenore can acknowledge the tremendous frustration she feels when, once again at her job, she receives a less than optimal evaluation, and in pondering her work behaviors glimpses the larger emotional themes in her life that would benefit from the experienced input of a therapist.

Some individuals turn to a self-therapy technique called *focusing*, originated by Eugene Gendlin (1981) at the University of Chicago. Not only are feelings contacted in this step-by-step process, but internal body awareness is also activated. By tuning in to this "felt sense" and communicating with it, tension is not only released but steps toward change also are identified through communications regarding what this awareness needs in order to bring the issue to beneficial resolution. In so doing, the wisdom of the body, emotions, and the mind are brought together in holistic fashion. The targeted predicament may take many rounds of focusing; however, with each round, the individual moves into a deeper knowing of the self in relation to the issue and opens up a new relationship with both emotions and the body. For those at ease with working on their own, this approach carries great merit.

So we see how the frontal cortex brings reality and reasoning to emotion. We know how the frontal cortex is ready and waiting to make healthier neural connections. Yet, as we saw earlier, the reasoning department is not asked for its opinion in emotional emergencies, nor is it infallible: false belief systems can create static in brain circuitry and produce faulty reasoning. Roxanne may believe alcohol is the only thing that can soothe her nerves, so when she starts to feel anxious, the belief supports her hand reaching for the bottle.

Deep down, Richard may believe he doesn't deserve the lead acting role, so when he feels a hint of anger at being passed over, he quiets it with rationalizations of why he wouldn't have done it justice after all. Richard's example shows us how *faulty thinking and the less mature defense mechanisms are one and the same*, both involving self-deception.

The use of projection is another case in point. When Teresa fixates on her belief that Barbara is too self-centered because she wears her accomplishments on her sleeve, it keeps her from being honest about how her own lack of discipline prevents similar accomplishments. Teresa believes she is "above" calling attention to herself, while underneath she hungers for acclaim. The day Teresa reverses her projection onto Barbara and owns her need for recognition, her cells of cognition can come to the rescue with suggestions as to how to proceed. She can begin to form neural connections through thought and imagery that promote self-expression.

Jeremy's penchant for shoplifting and stealing from street vendors stems from a false belief that the world owes him something. His acting out behaviors cover the grief and anger of an emotionally desolate childhood. As Jeremy owns the truth of his underlying emotions, his belief structure shifts from what is owed to him to what he owes himself.

Anger

Of all the emotions we relate to, anger is undoubtedly the most problematic of all, both individually and collectively. Just as anger provides the energy to fight or flee for physical survival, it plays an equally important role in our psychological health. No longer do we live in a jungle surrounded by tigers about to pounce from trees but in a jungle of political deception, technical challenge, commercial seduction, and relationship intrigue that we often perceive as imminently endangering to our self-worth. These more sophisticated jungle encounters—sometimes just as adrenalin charged as those of our forebears—do not find release through physical fight or flight.

We stew in our juices instead. Anger builds on anger, and when not informed by reason, trips an emotional emergency in the direction of violence; road rage is a perfect example. Research clearly indicates that people who habitually vent their anger in destructive ways strengthen their proclivity to do so every time they rage. Anger management programs that call on frontal cortex functioning for cognitive insights are the treatment of choice for such individuals. Mental health clinicians are now well aware of how assertiveness techniques, journal writing, role playing, and even colorful illustrations committed to paper constitute healthy ways of expressing anger while also providing the much needed cognitive input.

However, the emotional catharsis and anger release techniques popularized in the 1960s usually did not help in the long run, because the frontal cortex functioning was not fully understood or utilized. As novel as the experience may have been to yell one's anger into a bucket and hopefully leave it there, too often the accompanying importance of recognizing underlying patterns and beliefs was ignored. For example, identifying and appropriately asserting one's needs contributes to the bucket not filling up in the first place. None of this diminishes the fact that the discharge of rage is sometimes a necessary and healing release; after a violation such as rape, for example. This brings us to the relationship between disempowerment and anger—a condition filling the chairs of many a psychotherapist's waiting room. While rage-aholics are plagued by a livewire connection to anger, some individuals have little or no connection to rightful rage. Growing up with the idea that anger is wrong, lacking the modeling of healthy assertiveness, leaves more than a few of us empty handed. Afraid of anger in others and afraid of our own, accommodating and compliant behaviors stifle rightful assertion.

Remember that emotion informs. After repeated beatings from her husband, Megan one day decides she can no longer remain subject to the abuse, and anger mobilizes her to make the call to the women's shelter. Year after year of giving into his wife's unreasonable demands, Jared's frustration reaches the point of awareness, and he informs her they either go to counseling or he will leave. Whatever the outcome, his anger energized him to take the first step in breaking a dead-end pattern. Therapists have endless stories of individuals who feel disempowered. Fearing underlying aggression, unaided by the oozing leaks of passive-aggressive actions that do nothing to improve the situation, and believing that anger is bad keep individuals from connecting with the wisdom of the emotion, and their anger remains quarantined at a molecular level.

Whether a rage-aholic, anger repressor, or somewhere in between, the healing sequence is the same: awareness yoked to cognition. The rage-aholic, in recognizing anger's grip, can choose a time-out and experiment with various ways of cooling down. Equally important is challenging the thoughts that fuel rage in the first place, and professional assistance frequently is imperative.

On the other hand, the repressor's awareness often begins with an inventory of events that would normally evoke anger, noting customary responses: Did I brush that insult off? Did I ignore being cheated? When am I aware of hints of anger inside myself? The responsibility of awakening to buried anger includes learning approaches for healthy release and assertiveness that may involve assertiveness training and the aid of a competent counselor, or both.

Now back to Kevin to see how he is connecting his anger to his frontal lobes. Giving it his full attention, Kevin may talk his anger-packed dilemma over with a trusted friend, write it down on paper, or seek professional advice.

Kevin desires to reap the reward of anger connected with reason and welcomes the message anger has to give: addressing the unfinished business with his friend, with appropriate, reasoned input, could rescue this endangered relationship or bring it to its proper closure. Realizing that his friend does not have his side of the story, Kevin ponders the first step in taking action (which could include confronting the friend in a fitting manner, writing a letter, engaging in mediation, or working with a coach on communication techniques). This is responsible anger management. In so doing, the presence of anger molecules that reached consciousness are given their proper due. Kevin knew he was angry because he had been betrayed.

From there he dialed forward to his cortex, connecting his anger with the organizing, sorting, and problem-solving capacities of the brain. You can rightfully imagine a far different outcome if he had blindly acted on his first urge in the supermarket. Instead, Kevin activated the circuitry between the midbrain and the forebrain while strengthening his capacity for handling such emotional challenges more effectively, backed by new neuronal connections.

When emotion is connected to reason, we use a wiser moment to decide if now is the time to respond to an offense or if tomorrow would offer a clearer mindset. We choose to put job worries aside to spend quality time with family and friends. We pause to remember how crying is healthier than pushing back the tears. We remind ourselves that a strong feeling is not the problem, but the harmful reaction is. We understand that we need thinking intelligence *and* emotional intelligence. And of the two, as Goleman (1995) so memorably says, "Emotional intelligence adds far more of the qualities that make us more fully human" (p. 45).

This statement echoes back to what we already know about how an infant develops its "self" from the emotional communication it has with caregivers. It also resonates with the truth of how it is emotion that makes us feel alive. And in its completeness, this statement empowers the knowing that with each emotional dilemma we plug in to good reason with the promotion of new neural connections, we bring ourselves closer to wholeness—and hopefully bring those touched by our efforts along.

Professional Help And Other Considerations

In this fascinating era of self-help books, support groups, consciousness raising workshops, and psychologically oriented talk shows, we have much to pick and choose from without ever consulting a psychotherapist, unless that be the route we prefer and one that produces desired results. At the same time, sporadically I have made suggestions about seeking professional help in regard to specific dilemmas. This is with good reason. The line between self-help and expert assistance is often drawn by the degree to which we are subject to emotional hijacking. This line divides those living in a state of honest, informed self-expression with the least amount of harm to self and others, from those driven by emotional emergencies, ritualistic behaviors, or crippled communications that demoralize self and others. If you are discovering that emotional volatility and psychological dysfunction overshadow many of your interactions, professional help is advised. See Appendix C for assistance in locating a psychotherapist.

For many of us, the experience of a therapeutic alliance can provide an essential catalyst for growth at certain junctures along the way.

Psychotherapists are trained to see our blind spots and reflect insights back to us in nonthreatening ways. Fortunately, the stigma attached to the "shrink's" office is weakening, no longer a signal that the visitor is crazed or in need of hospitalization. Not only is mental health gaining momentum, the field of psychotherapeutics is increasingly lending itself to scientific evaluation. The aforementioned Eye Movement Desensitization and Reprocessing (EMDR) technique is a case in point. Based on the assumption that emotional trauma results in a brain imprint that skews cognitive reasoning, EMDR is said to access a natural processing network that moves information to an adaptive resolution—another way of saying a clearer connection is being fashioned between the midbrain and forebrain with stimulation of the growth of new neurons between synapses. Research protocols indicate the efficacy of this technique. While not effective in every case, EMDR can decrease emotional hijacking, diminish anxiety, and further one along the path of growing up the ego.

Other therapeutic approaches can be equally valuable—traditional verbal psychotherapy, Ericksonian hypnosis, biofeedback, psychodrama, renegotiation trauma therapy, to name but a few. Also of benefit, especially in combination with therapeutic processes, are hands-on modalities (massage, Alexander Technique, Ruebenfeld, Feldenkries, Therapeutic Touch, and numerous others) that communicate directly with cells holding molecules of emotions in the body. How we go about choosing a body worker is as important as the manner in which we choose a psychotherapist. Training, experience, philosophy, style, the "feel" of the match, and ethics all factor into the decision.

The healing path that suits one person may be a total misfit for another. In addition, the approach that was a match at one point along the way may no longer serve an individual's purpose, begging to be replaced by another.

Sometimes it is a matter of going to the self-help section of a bookstore and seeing what leaps out from the shelf. Sometimes it is a matter of picking up a clue from another's conversation. Sometimes it is a simple yet powerful matter of responding to your own intuitive hints.

Because self-help approaches are vast in number and varied in technique, it can be difficult to sort through the maze. I would like to mention a few found to be significant when integrated into therapy or even when crafted on one's own.

Meditation

This is a way of meditation— self-styled to fix attention on a specific emotion to the exclusion of all other thoughts or feeling states. This objectifying of emotion diminishes judgment, empties our minds of the extraneous, and allows new perceptions to surface. Gendlin's focusing technique (see p. 85) is similarly contemplative.

Of course, meditation in the traditional sense involves quieting the nervous system by holding a specific thought, image, or word in the mind and returning to it (or repeating it) over and over again. In addition to its spiritual value, the benefit of meditation to the health of our bodies and minds is reaching unprecedented status, especially as the accumulation of scientific evidence endorses its positive effects. The Centerpointe Research Institute (www.centerpointe.com) provides information as to how their technology gives the brain a stimulus that creates new neural connections between the left and right hemispheres of the brain. Indeed, the distance between Eastern and Western healing approaches is shrinking!

Christopher Germer's book, *The Mindful Path to Self-Compassion*(2009), is a premier example of a scientifically based meditative approach. Instead of resisting and fighting difficult emotions, psychologist Germer presents a step- bystep guide for bearing witness to pain and directing loving kindness to the experience of it. For example, among the many practical exercises is one using the acronym **FACE**:

Earlier in the "Say Hello to Your Emotions" section, I suggested questions we can bring to a feeling state. (What is its feel? Where in the body do I feel it? What is its shape? What is it made

- ◊ **F**eel the pain
- ◊ **A**ccept it
- ◊ **C**ompassionately respond
- ◊ **E**xpect skillful action

Because Germer's book so scientifically and pragmatically touches the very nexus of the science of self-nurturing and how this involves acceptance and right use of emotion, you may well find it a valuable adjunct to your progression through the ego-growth stages.

Self-soothing activity, as suggested in Exercise 5.d (chapter 5). If you are not applying such activities on a regular basis, write down why. No matter how regular the use, write down the emotions you experience when you are successfully engaged in self-nurturing activity.

The Enneagram

Originating from the ancient tradition of Sufism, the Enneagram is a symbology of personality that describes nine personality types with nine levels of development within each type. Students of the Enneagram become observers of their internal maps (including the use of defense mechanisms) and make choices of new behaviors, just as you are doing in this work. A number of years ago when I first discovered my "point" on the Enneagram, the perfectionist, I was astonished to read descriptions of my internal patterns I had never seen in print before. A powerful tool, the Enneagram deepens understanding of human nature and broadens appreciation of differences among personality types. Furthermore, it strengthens motivation for reaching the next stage of personal growth, which from the Enneagram perspective, ultimately leads to spiritual realization (thus sharing the same purpose as this book). If you so choose, the Enneagram can be a beneficial support to maturing your ego, and in particular, can help identify and validate the primary issues that form the pillars intersecting your growth spiral.

Exercise 6.i

Review your progress with the use of the comforting,

Exercise 6.j

Choose to be very aware of the next encounter you have with a distressing emotion, be it fear, anger, jealousy, sadness, or whatever. Consciously greet this emotion by naming it—saying it aloud or silently to yourself and, if possible, writing it down. Next take a deep breath and ask the emotion what it needs.

- ◊ Does it need appropriate and healthy expression? ◊ Does it need to be listened to by your support person?
- ◊ Does it need to know what options exist regarding its expression?
- ◊ Does it say it needs to be immediately expressed, no matter the outcome?

If such is the case, tell the emotion you are very aware of the high level of distress and at the same time you are committed to helping the energy of the emotion to be expressed in the most healthy of ways. If you are in a situation that does not allow you to give immediate attention to it, tell the emotion exactly when you will give it your focus, and make sure that you follow through.

It's also important to remember that a time out from such situations is very appropriate, as it gives you time to listen to and negotiate with the emotion and strongly increases the potential for a favorable resolution to the distress.

Summing It All Up

When you first committed to growing up your ego, the playing field was broad and the boundaries uncircumscribed. Not knowing what topics would be covered, what data would be integrated, or what would be of interest to you, you took the plunge and impressed your brain with an array of facts and ideas. Whether committed to paper or not, in one way or another you pondered responses to the questions and exercises about your behaviors and attitudes. Things were and are coming together.

Now you have added a mass of information that reaches right into the heart of the matter and into the heart of you! Remember how the heart is home to every neuropeptide receptor and not just a metaphor for how we hold our hands over our hearts when we say such things as: "It feels like a knife in my heart"; "I feel love for you"; "My heart is broken." How the energy of emotion does or does not flow through you is analogous to the rhythm of your heart beating life into every cell of your body. No uncertainty exists regarding the rhythm of a healthy heart. No uncertainty exists regarding what science has to say about the integrity of emotions. No uncertainty exists regarding the mind-body connection. No uncertainty exists regarding how our brains evolve and have the capacity to transform dysfunction into emotional integrity. With body and mind in synchronicity, the heart beats to the emotional and spiritual rhythm of love—love of myself, love of everyone, and love of all creation.

Congratulations for reaching this point. Whether or not you believe you are progressing or making conscious use of what you are reading, your brain continues to absorb what is relevant for you. It may be today, or a week, a month, or a year from now when your consciousness informs you it is time to commune with you about what you're learning or have learned as you've read. Then you can go about applying the truth that is yours in your own way and at your own pace.

We're into the homestretch now. In the next chapter you will learn more about the role of emotion in getting to know and integrate your shadow side. And you already know about the last two chapters—the dessert of this book with delicious emotional and spiritual renderings of what it means and how it looks to be all ego-grown-up!

WORKS CITED

Amen, D. G. (1998). *Change your brain, change your life.* New York: Three Rivers Press.

Darwin, C. (1872). *The expression of emotions in man and animals.* Reprinted by the University of Chicago Press (1965).

Dispenza, J. (2007). *Evolve your brain: The science of changing your mind.* Deerfield, FL: Health Communications, Inc.

Gendlin, E. T. (1981). *Focusing.* New York: Bantam Books.

Germer, C. K. (2009). *The mindful path to selfcompassion: Freeing yourself from destructive thoughts and emotions.* New York: Guilford Press.

Goleman, D. (1995). *Emotional intelligence.* New York: Bantam Books.

LeDoux, J. (1996). *The emotional brain: The mysterious underpinnings of emotional life.* New York: Simon & Schuster.

Pert, C. (1997). *Molecules of emotion.* New York: Simon & Schuster.

Obstacles to Growth

Any depiction of ego growth would not be complete without careful consideration of two potent stumbling blocks: the shadow self of repressed emotional energy and the phenomenon of paradox. Although closely related, each has its own distinctive manner in hindering ultimate achievement of the highest stages. While the shadow waits for us to turn around and look at it, paradox leaves no stone unturned in its obvious presentation. We begin with the shadow hidden from view and close the chapter with the mystery and challenge of contradiction.

The Shadow Self

Whether constant or sporadic, repressed parts of ourselves—the shadow self—can often be the cause of problematic and hurtful emotional maneuvers that produce feelings of aloneness and periods of social isolation. What hides from our conscious awareness in our unconscious minds can stir up a great deal of trouble, and because we don't know where it comes from, we tend to blame others and wallow in our misery. This masked and potent energy can sabotage our best efforts, fuel behaviors that shock us ("That's not the real me that did that!"), and haunt us in dreams throughout the night.

Being gripped by shadow material is directly related to how very proficient we are at holding on to beliefs and behaviors that don't serve us well. Perhaps an underlying attitude of unworthiness results in a victim stance or unconscious guilt keeps an individual frozen in a constant and draining caregiving role. Growing up the ego means that, in spite of the role of defense mechanisms to keep tension at bay, our task is to challenge the status quo by looking at the shadow cast by detrimental behaviors. The major defense mechanism the shadow self uses to make itself known is projection, although few people understand that what we don't like in another person may be mirroring something hidden in ourselves.

In this chapter we are going to explore how in its various manifestations the shadow self comes into being, how you can identify your shadow even as you go about your daily affairs, and how you can befriend it so that it works with you instead of against you. You will not only learn about the shadow's intimate relationship with projection but also about the inner workings of this defense mechanism so you can responsibly bring its energy back home for use as an ego-growth tool.

The Shadow Comes Into Being

Every child naturally develops a shadow. In recalling the evolution of the developmental stages, it is easy to see that what is considered "good" by Mom, Dad, and other caretakers becomes the ego ideal—what I should be or want to be in order to make the right impression on people and supposedly get the best out of life. Forming a "good" self is not only necessary for survival (as we learned in chapter 3), it is also a way to get praise and to feel self-satisfied.

Poet Robert Bly's (1988) illustration of how the shadow comes into being goes back to his childhood, when he likens him and his brother to radiating balls of energy.

We had a ball of energy, all right; but one day we noticed that our parents didn't like certain parts of that ball. They said things like: "Can't you be still?" or "It isn't nice to try and kill your brother." Behind us we have an invisible bag, and the part of us our parents don't like, we, to keep our parents' love, put in the bag. By the time we go to school our bag is quite large (p. 17).

That bag is our personal shadow, and by young adulthood, a lot of repressed energy is dragging behind us. The repressed energy that goes into the shadow is everything that did not fit our ego ideal. In some environments greed is frowned upon, in others sexuality is taboo. In many families the expression of anger is not allowed, and in some a lid is put on creativity and spontaneity, so that potentially positive energy is also confined within the shadow. The bottom line is that the energy of all that is put into shadow abets the dark side of human nature, including our undeveloped talents and gifts.

Remember that scientists have discovered the vital contribution emotions make to healthy living, making no distinction between positive and negative ones. *What occurs as a result of how our emotions are handled makes the difference.* Hiding them away causes them to ferment. Over time, shadow energy regresses to a more primitive level, becomes hostile to us, and undermines what we do. This energy wants rightful recognition and use, for it carries compelling life forces and resorts to all kinds of indirect means to make itself known and express that energy. For example, the perpetually calm librarian who flies into an alarming rage hasn't yet figured out that beneath her relaxed demeanor is a woman who hates her job. Such an eruption is her shadow knocking at the door of consciousness, with the invitation to stop compromising one's self. Whether shadow presents itself through startling behaviors, dreams, snarled relationships, or whatever else, it brings us a fertile opportunity to unveil its dynamics and to learn how the charge of such buried emotions can be creatively transformed.

At the same time, the relationship we need to cultivate with our shadow is long-term, with mysterious parts of ourselves—which defense mechanisms work hard to conceal—that must be coaxed out of the dark over and over again. Gradually, a more conscious relationship is established with the shadow, and as psychotherapists Connie Zweig and Steve Wolf (1997) comment, "When shadow work is attended to, the soul feels round, full . . . welcomed, alive in the gardens, aroused in passion, awake in sacred things" (p. 9). These words provide an inspiring description of the results of bringing shadow content to light, as such efforts intertwine with and contribute to the fruits of ego-growth work.

Preparing To Do Shadow Work

Identifying the shadow self *is* the doorway to our uniqueness because the shadow surely holds creativity, power, and vigor, without which we cannot grow up our egos and be truly whole. Take the example of an individual whose artistic talent was buried early on by disapproving parents who made sure their son established himself in a professional career. In so doing, this young man's shadow collected a great deal of raw and unprocessed energy. We can imagine in his adulthood the pull he would feel toward the creative realm that would take him to a gallery, a painting class, or to the art section of a bookstore, whetting his appetite but allowing nothing more. He may be like many who believe it is impossible, impractical, and even absurd to pay attention to deeper yearnings that might change one's life.

Yes, dealing with shadow material will change your life, but it doesn't necessarily mean a vast reconstruction. Frequently, ongoing revisions make room for shadow material as we give committed attention to its cues and respond with gradual and ongoing changes. Nevertheless, it is important to keep in mind that, when tapping into the unconscious mind, we are dealing with deep and profound forces. Appropriate safeguards must be in place.

These safeguards include a cautious and respectful attitude, a gentle approach, and willingness to work at a slow pace, for shadow energy becomes reactive when hard-pressed.

Furthermore, central to shadow processing and the taking back of projection is the need for a strong base of support, the core of which is your ability to self-nurture. All that you learned in chapter 5 about the internalization of a holding environment and the work that you have done to anchor your ability to hold yourself secure will be of much help here. In addition, calling on your support person, if you have one in place, or interacting with your wiser self through written word is very much in order.

An additional safeguard is to contract with yourself that if shadow and projection work in any way trigger feelings that overwhelm you (such as anxiety, fear, sadness, anger, confusion, etc.), you will make an appointment with a therapist—this may be one of those junctures when professional help is an essential choice. This is especially true for those with a past history of physical or sexual abuse or severe emotional and spiritual abuse. It is also true for those who suffered serious deficits during the time of infant bonding or who have post-traumatic stress disorder. If you fall into any of these categories, or if you have been diagnosed with a mental disorder and you are not presently in therapy with a licensed mental health practitioner, availing yourself of such assistance is the recommended route. (See Appendix C for information regarding mental health community resources.)

Exercise 7.a

- ◊ What safeguards do you have in place for shadow and projection work?
- ◊ Are you prepared to ask for professional help should you need it?

Projection

We first take a look at the role of projection in mirroring the shadow and the opportunity it gives us to become more acquainted with what it has to reveal. From chapter 4, we know that projection falls into the category of an immature defense mechanism and occurs when the traits we dislike in others are those we don't like and can't accept in ourselves. The mechanism of projection is a particularly weighty defense in keeping individuals tied to the conformist stage. At the same time, due to its subtlety and close relationship to the shadow, it can also be seen tagging along into the sixth and seventh stages of ego growth.

When we attribute our unacceptable impulses to others or blame them for our personal failures, projection can justify prejudice and discard accountability. The use of this defense mechanism runs rampant in our society—just listen to conversations in a bar, in an airplane terminal, or wherever people congregate and talk. You'll hear story after story of what so-and-so did or did not do to or for the other person, what was said or not said, and the overriding exasperation with it all. When the underlying defense in these tales is projection, no real slack is given for human nature or for what the offending person's situation might be, and no serious consideration is paid to how the offended person might have contributed to the dilemma.

For instance, in a small sandwich shop, a typical conversation you might overhear at the next table sounds like this: a man tells a woman about a telephone call he received from a friend ("not a very close one at that, mind you"), who asked if she could borrow some money. "It didn't take me long to let her know in an exasperated way that I have no extra dollars floating around to lend out to anyone—let alone her, although I didn't say that last part to her. I know what she does with her time and money: she wastes both. I wouldn't think of being that irresponsible. I bet she wanted money from me to go to one of those writing workshops she loves, even when she has to skip work to attend. I'm not like that. I go to work every day, put in my hours, collect an honest paycheck, and feel good about it. Work before play is what I always say."

It's easy to see the black-and-white thinking of this man, and to know that conforming behavior is important to him. He doesn't extend his perspective beyond his own belief system or way of doing things. No doubt, it never occurred to him that his indignation may have been ignited by a part of his being that longs to play, to throw caution to the wind, and to become a free spirit. The strong possibility exists that what this man dislikes in his friend is exactly what he can't allow in himself and would condemn within himself were he to become aware of it. Among other things, projection creates separation between people while closing the door to true sharing. In the above example, the man obviously missed the cue that his resentment was providing an opportunity for inner exploration. Furthermore, no matter what the reason for not lending the money, there are softer and kinder ways to decline.

Projection operates in larger arenas, often with dire consequences. In families, it can be an extremely dysfunctional thorn in ongoing dynamics, sometimes causing relatives not to speak to each other for decades. One family that came to me some years ago was so completely caught up in projection, the family-run business was about to go under. The oldest son, who was to be the "heir" to the directorship of the company, was described by the father as a "ne'er-do-well," drinking all the time, and worst of all, "chasing every skirt that went by the door." The son referred to his father as "the Gestapo," stating that his father expected him to work a sixty-hour week while never giving him any strokes for anything he did well. The mother, caught in the middle, said very little because, as bookkeeper, she said, "I just keep my nose in the ledger and don't pay attention to what's going on otherwise." The younger daughter, on the other hand, was furious because she worked as hard as she could for the company, got little notice from the mother and father, and resented all the hoopla her brother caused. She thought she should be the director of the company when her father retired and had not spoken to her brother directly for several months, communicating with him at work via e-mail.

The family prematurely left therapy after just three sessions. I later heard their business collapsed following the father's heart attack. I couldn't help but wonder had they gotten to the place of exploring the father's background—the values placed on him and what he might have felt he was missing in his life—if a chunk of projection might have started to lift. By the same token, if the son could have gotten in touch with the part of himself that had a more responsible streak, the question could have been posed as to whether he really wanted to work in the family business or apply himself to a vocation for which he was better suited. One could speculate about the favorable impact such conversations and possibilities might have had on his sister.

The father was projecting disowned lechery onto his son, and the son was projecting his disowned responsibility onto his father. Here is where the subtlety and trickiness of projection shows itself. Yes, the son was irresponsible, which gave the father a bell to ring. And yes, the father was a driving dictator who gave the son good fat to chew on. Yet the challenge of growth is to place the focus inward and ferret out those feelings and reactions activated by situations and individuals outside ourselves and dig for the gold of deeper truth. Then in circumstances such as this one, the risk of sharing personal realizations might open new doors of communication and acceptance between the individuals involved, not to mention the freeing of energy for healthier pursuits.

As you will soon see in the next section, loosening the grip of projection involves persistent awareness, strength to look at the unsavory, and willingness to change—all dynamic work for the ego-growth warrior and warrioress.

Exercise 7.b

One of the best ways for discovering how projection operates in our lives comes from Jungian analyst William A. Miller (1991) and involves making a list of all the characteristics you do not like in other people. Begin by thinking about people who annoy and anger you or about instances of frustration with others, even strangers. As quickly as possible, write down the offensive traits: greed, selfishness, laziness, rigidity, whatever comes up for you. Don't expect this to be a short list. Take your time and allow yourself days or weeks. When you feel the inventory is complete, put a star µ next to those qualities that you actually hate.

Make a new list of these starred items and you will have a fairly good sketch of your individual shadow material. What you have before you may shock you, and you may find it hard to accept. Try to avoid criticizing yourself.

The next step is to examine your behavior to see if you, at least at times, exhibit the same characteristic. For example, if laziness is one of the starred items, for one week observe in yourself any tendency toward slacking off, being distracted by "more interesting things," or daydreaming your time away. If such periods occur, note how often and what you are feeling in those moments. As difficult and jarring as this may be, you are in the thick of owning your projection, doing ego-growth work. The next time feelings of judgment and loathing come up when you witness laziness in another, bring your awareness back to your own penchant for such behavior.

The challenge is not to put yourself down for this characteristic but rather to appreciate what you are learning about your shadow and your humanness. While not all judgments and criticisms are projections, it is important to note that whenever we emotionally overreact to another person's behavior, something in the shadow is being triggered and is asking for attention. In a later section we will look at various ways for dealing with and befriending shadow material.

Remember that emotions are not good or bad, and that the shadow carries every possibility—from hatred and revenge to kindness and forgiveness. It may be hard to imagine kindness would be stuffed away, but some children are not modeled such a quality or may be taught to be suspicious of everything and everybody in their world. In this kind of situation, projection may show itself through an individual idolizing or falling in love with someone who shows kindness even if in a limited way, while believing she could never show that capacity herself. Far to the contrary, the energy of benevolence and generosity are in her shadow waiting to be known.

Exercise 7.c

Refer to the list you've begun in your journal (per instructions on this page, Exercise 7.b). Choose one example from this list and write about it in more detail. Call on memories of past situations when you experienced the same adverse characteristic in other people. Appreciate how this deeper exploration will increase your understanding of the presence of this characteristic in your life, including insights regarding how and why you have kept yourself from identifying this trait as residing in yourself.

Looking through the Window

Another way of encountering our projections and shadow self involves examining the fixed notions we have of ourselves that don't always match up with how the world sees us. The Johari window—a metaphorical window divided into four segments, each pane reflecting a specific aspect of the self—exemplifies how this works. *Quadrant one* represents the self I show to others (my persona). *Quadrant two* represents the self known only to me (my secrets). *Quadrant three* represents what others see about me that I don't see (my blind spot). *Quadrant four* represents what neither others nor I know about myself (unknown potentials/ what is unconscious).

Sometimes a specific quadrant outsizes the others—quadrant two with its personal secrets may occupy the bulk of the window as in the case of a bigamist. Quadrant one is not only the face we present to the world, but also includes the degree to which a person presents a front seemingly at odds with what lies underneath, such as when we sense anger or frustration behind another's "sweet" smile. And of course, quadrant four's unknown contents buried deep in the psyche are not currently available to me or to those who observe me.

Our present focal point is quadrant three, because it signals shadow material often manifested through projection. This pane framing our blind spots is directly related to faulty beliefs about ourselves that drive certain behaviors. How scary it can be to realize that others see things about ourselves we don't see at all! It goes like this: "Max has a blind spot—he just doesn't get it that while he complains all the time about people who tell anecdotes they've told many times over, he has his own version of controlling conversations that keeps us all squirming. Why doesn't he snap to it?" Max believes he isn't a controller, and overtly he does not come across as a power monger. Nonetheless, with passive aggressive aplomb, he detains and bores others with lengthy accounts of daily trivia.

Sometimes others clue us in, gently or otherwise, about our blind spots and accompanying false beliefs. Agonizing as this is, it is a valuable opportunity to explore the shadow for whatever nugget of truth is relevant to our growth. At the same time, when we receive faultfinding information about ourselves from another, it is helpful to keep the following in mind:

1. Remind yourself that an initial defensive reaction is normal. To the best of your ability, observe the upsurge of feeling within yourself without judging it; just allow it to be while remaining quiet.
2. Take the time you need to verbally reflect back to the person what was said to make sure you heard the information correctly. Unless you can calmly explore the issue further (and only if you have the desire to do so), the conversation can end at that point with "I will think about what you've said."

3. Realize that the information comes through the subjective filter of another's perception. Through personal reflection, self-observation, and perhaps even checking the information out with a trusted friend or counselor, you can decide what is shadow truth and what is not.

When I was confronted during my marriage about the amount of time I was spending on a civil rights project that my husband perceived as taking too much time away from the children, I was shocked and distraught. He had, up to that point, supported my efforts toward this cause. Nonetheless, I didn't have to check out his view with anyone, for after several days of reflection and observation, I knew what he was saying to be true. In making the choice to reduce the amount of time with the organization, it not only provided more time with my children, it also gave me the opportunity to explore my priorities, along with the hidden aspects of why I became so markedly involved in the project in the first place. Over time, I realized how my "serving behaviors," at least in part, fed my ego ideal—the view I had of myself as a generous giver of time and energy to people in need. The problem was that I shortchanged not only my children but also myself, for there was little time or space for consideration of my own personal needs—needs that waited in the shadow to be known and met.

This "blind spot" windowpane pops open over and over again in our dealings with others, particularly in close or intimate relationships where disagreements are inevitable. When occasions of conflict present themselves, we have the choice to defensively hold on to our position 100 percent or remember Johari and listen for whatever slice of truth should rightfully be heard. The movie, *In the Bedroom,* is peppered from the beginning with instances of the wife's controlling and unforgiving tendencies. When her husband, in a fit of frustration and fury, blurts this out to her, she remains silent and eventually acknowledges the forthrightness of what she hears.

Without going into the twists that fuel the rest of the tale, this woman's brush with reality leaves many a viewer surprised by her accepting response. In short, while criticism may include a good dose of projection, more often than not it carries at least a sliver of truth about ourselves.

Exercise 7.d

In your journal, draw the Johari window (see p. 99) and label each pane. In the "what others see and I don't see" pane, write down a word or phrase referring to the last time you received criticism from someone. Think about it for several days. Then make a full journal entry exploring what nugget of truth may be contained in the criticism and how that reflects a shadow characteristic. Note if it is included in the list you made in Exercise 7.b (p. 98).

Befriending The Shadow

Befriending the shadow is demanding and complex. The aspects of ourselves we've relegated to the darkness aren't naturally friendly, nor are they easy to accept as belonging to ourselves. For all of us, the bottom line of psychological and spiritual wholeness, and thus ego maturity, means learning to love ourselves in our entirety. To the degree we are lacking in that capacity, what we banish, judge, or ignore within us will not only sabotage many of our best efforts, the secret and the hidden will also block our capacity for truly loving others. We have already seen how our disowned qualities create distance and separation when we experience those very characteristics in others. The effects of projection in intimate relationships are vast and often destructive, leading many a couple to divorce court. The shadow also hangs out in our addictions, hides in our private shames, leaks out in cruel humor, may erupt during midlife, and can mask itself in physical symptoms.

To discover the underbelly of our sexuality, our aggression, our greed, our grief, or whatever our shadow traits may be, is a very humbling experience and may produce strong feelings of repulsion. Again, that's why making acquaintance with your shadow contents must be approached cautiously and with the understanding that this is an involved and, most likely, a lifelong project. Think of how you would handle a situation in which an antagonist in your life ended up on your work team. As manager of the team, it would be your responsibility to figure out a way to incorporate his personality and abilities as smoothly as possible. Hopefully, you wouldn't say to the others on the team that this guy is trouble, or call him individually into your office to issue all kinds of warnings based on his past behavior. If you are wise enough, you will go about this in a reflective and indirect manner, taking time to observe how he functions in this new situation while directing his strengths to tasks more apt to build a favorable reputation. Then the hurdles that come along stand a better chance of being manageable. Not only have you broadened your perspective of him by your approach, this experience may open the door to a more cooperative relationship.

So it is with shadow material. We want to approach it with a reflective and curious attitude— not by trying to break through the door of darkness but by peeking through the window with a flashlight. Numerous ways exist to do this, as you will discover in what follows.

The Round Table

One of the best techniques for making acquaintance with shadow material I learned from Jungian analyst Robert Johnson (1986), when he spoke at a local college some years ago. Using a personal example from his own experience, Johnson described a period of unrest he had gone through in regard to his professional life. In his pondering, he couldn't quite get to the bottom of what was making him feel so unsettled. Nothing seemed to click. So he decided to try to contact this part of his shadow self by using active imagination—in this case, an imagined conversation with his shadow—an approach he outlined in his book, *Inner Work: Using Dreams and Active Imagination for Personal Growth*. As he described this technique to the audience, he pointed out how doing this on a typewriter (or computer) involves switching from lower case to upper case, lower case being the conscious mind and upper case being the shadow part. (I have found it can also be done through writing by hand—the dominant hand being the conscious mind and the nondominant hand being the shadow part.)

To emphasize how these discussions with shadow parts best unfold, Johnson said they must be conducted as though seated at a round table. No part is superior to another part. Listening and negotiating are the avenues to connecting and integrating. In Johnson's case the dialogue concerning his restlessness revealed a secret part that was very upset with how much he worked and was insisting he "play" more. When Johnson told his shadow part he understood his frustration and demands, he also said he was willing to do something about it. The shadow part said he wanted to go to Tahiti where he knew there were attractive native women. Johnson replied that his present schedule did not allow for such a foray, but he was willing to adjust his time in the present to accommodate some aspect of play. For starters and through negotiation, it was agreed that one night a week Johnson would close his office early and go to a drive-in movie. Johnson didn't go on from there regarding the evolution of more play in his life, but his example shows how, when encountering a shadow self, communication is not only possible, negotiation opens the window to new behaviors allowing gradual and appropriate assimilation of what heretofore had been outlawed.

How can you initiate such a dialogue? Begin by announcing your presence (dominant hand or lower case) and asking the part that is involved in your dilemma if it would be willing to speak with you. Here is an example:

Sue: I am here and would like to talk to the part of me that stirs up massive anxiety when my sister-in-law visits.

Responder: I HEAR YOU.
thank you. i would like to talk more with you.

WHAT DO YOU WANT?
i want to know why the anxiety happens. I DON'T LIKE HER.

Why? she's nice enough and tries to be considerate of our family schedule.
SHE MAY BE NICE, BUT YOU'RE TOO NICE BACK TO HER.

what do you mean?

YOU WORRY TOO MUCH ABOUT WHETHER YOU'RE PLEASING HER. YOU DO THE SAME THING WITH LOTS OF PEOPLE.

oh, i'll have to think about that.

REMEMBER THE TIME SHE SPILLED SPAGHETTI SAUCE ALL OVER THE FLOOR? YOU WERE REALLY MAD, BUT YOU JUST SMILED AND MOPPED IT UP. I WANTED TO BOP HER A GOOD ONE FOR JUST SITTING THERE AND WATCHING YOU DO THE WORK. I GET REALLY TIRED OF THAT SMILE OF YOURS THAT COVERS UP YOUR IRRITATIONS.

you think i'm too nice.

YOU'RE ALWAYS PAYING ATTENTION TO WHAT EVERBODY ELSE WANTS AND NEEDS. HERE I AM, THE PART OF YOU THAT WANTS TO TELL PEOPLE THE TRUTH.

so you feel left out.

YOU BET, AND IT'S TIME YOU STARTED PAYING ATTENTION TO ME.

what do you need?

I'M TIRED OF PLAYING SECOND FIDDLE. I WANT YOU TO CHECK IN WITH ME ABOUT WHAT I FEEL AND LET ME SAY WHAT'S ON MY MIND.

FOR EXAMPLE, I WOULD LIKE TO TELL THAT BITCH THAT SHE'S TOO SELF-CENTERED. SHE TALKS ABOUT HERSELF ALL THE TIME AND HARDLY EVER ASKS YOU ABOUT YOURSELF OR WHAT YOU WANT TO DO.

well, i'm not going to lash out like that. but i'm beginning to get your point. i need to think about all of this—it's rather shocking to hear what you have to say, but that's what I want to know. could we meet again and continue our talk? by the way, what should i call you?

CALL ME "TELLY"—TELL IT LIKE IT IS. AND WHEN WE TALK AGAIN, YOU BETTER BE ABLE TO GIVE ME AN EXAMPLE FROM THIS WEEK OF WHAT I DON'T LIKE ABOUT YOU.

i'll do my best.

In this example, the initial groundwork was laid for ongoing discussion and negotiation. Telly, the shadow part, is probably going to go for broke wanting Sue to become very in touch with her emotions and just as outspoken as possible in expressing them. As Sue becomes more aware of her underlying feelings, she and Telly will have to travel some sensitive territory together as they negotiate appropriate expression in regard to when, where, with whom, and to what degree she speaks her emotional truth.

Exercise 7.e

Choose one characteristic from Exercise 7.b (p. 98) and use the round table technique to learn more about this shadow quality and how you can create an alliance with it.

Keep in mind that this technique involves ongoing dialogues with the characteristic over time. This is how alliances comes into being as consideration, negotiation, and loving acceptance support the transformation and integration of this shadow aspect into the whole of you.

Dreams and Daydreams

The dreaming we do at night as well as the fantasies we entertain during the day are both laden with shadow material. Night dreaming is, as Freud told us, "the royal road to the unconscious," whereby the dark and the hidden can rise and have its say. Integral to increasing our self-awareness during the transition ego-growth stages is the attention we give our dreams and the energy spent exploring their meaning. The more seriously we take our dreams and the more we give them consideration, the more they reveal to us—a discipline that provides generous growth rewards.

The initial step in dream work often involves keeping a journal, recording the dream as soon as we can—preferably when we first wake from it, even in the middle of the night, if possible. In the beginning, trying to understand our dreams may be confusing and frustrating, seemingly filled with nonsensical images and activities that have little or nothing to do with ourselves. Over time and perhaps with the help of a dream group, an appropriate dream-interpretation book, or discussion with a therapist, themes emerge and meanings take form. I once had a client who, early in her therapy, reported a dream of her oldest brother being wrapped in a large plastic bag. Although alive, he lay motionless.

In our dialogue, it came to light that her brother had remained in a dysfunctional marriage out of guilt for an affair he had (which became public knowledge) some years prior. Initially, the woman thought the dream was just a reflection of her brother's sad state of affairs. Further discussion revealed more than that. When asked what part of herself her brother might represent, the conversation took a far different turn.

"Well," she said, "I suppose he represents some aspect of the masculine part of me, and that's not something I've dealt with very effectively."

Her brother, although a fairly successful businessman, was overpowered in his personal life by his wife. His affair was an attempt to call attention to the uncomfortable state of his marriage, but marital counseling did not seem to address the basic difficulties between the two. I asked her if there was a part of her life that gave her the feeling of being sealed up.

"Yes," she said, "it involves my inability to move forward with my dissertation. The chairman of my committee is very fixed in his ways, and I tend to clam up around him, just as I did with my father when he was alive— like the professor, he was rigid and controlling. I guess this dream is dealing with my lack of power and how fear keeps me trapped."

And so it was that this woman immersed herself in shadow work by first connecting with the part of her (a part that needed the masculine capacity for action and the handling of conflict) that was trapped in a way similar to her brother in his marital situation. Through dialogue and role-playing, she made acquaintance with the long-denied aggressive part of her nature. The work of allowing the energy of the aggression to show itself was not easy, nor did it occur within a few short sessions. However, as the gestalt of the energy rose in session work, she gradually negotiated the difference between the primitive aspect of the aggression that she discharged through spoken fantasy, and the appropriate and tempered use of such energy in daily reality. She not only grew to identify when anger and rage were stirring inside her, she eventually mastered the ability to partner with it in ways that helped her mission move forward. In working with shadow material that presented in a dream, this woman integrated a masculine part of herself that contributed greatly to her pursuit of wholeness.

Fantasies and daydreams can be treated much the same as dreams, first of all by giving them serious consideration as links to shadow material, and secondly by exploring the images and activities that come forward. David, a poetic kind of man, entertained a recurring fantasy of living in the woods where deer and coyote ambled by, and birds of many species gathered to sing their songs. In great detail he imagined the little house he would live in throughout the four seasons—the blue sky of summer with sunlight streaming through the window; the leaves drifting to the ground in the autumn; the snow of winter piled high against the north side of the house; and the magnificent green of spring creeping up through the earth. In the midst of relating this, tears filled his eyes. Replying to my inquiry as to what the sadness was all about, he remained quiet for some time before he described how, in childhood, his family vacationed each summer in a cottage in the woods. So enchanted was he with the place that he never wanted to leave, but his father yearly reminded him that when he grew up, he could have such a place of his own if he put his mind to it. "This fantasy is a direct connection to my father. He died five years ago, and I never let myself fully grieve his passing or think about how I experienced him as a father. He was an alcoholic until I was ten years old, and it was not a pretty picture. After he joined Alcoholics Anonymous and became sober, it was like getting a new dad. Yet, he and I never really talked about any of that stuff. He died with many words unspoken between the two of us. The house in the woods I dream of is like a solace, a representation of my father and the potential he saw in me and the potential I saw in our relationship."

Obviously, the fantasy tied in to David's shadow in several ways. It soothed him when bad memories of an abusing, alcoholic father threatened to break through, and it also strangely haunted him because it mirrored something to him he had not incorporated in his life—connection with nature in an ongoing and sustaining way. This fantasy served as a springboard to the shadow work of confronting the early truth of his relationship with his father, experiencing the grief he had stuffed away, and exploring how he could bring more of the outdoors into his life. This middle-aged man not only took on the challenge of what he had long denied, he actually went back to school and studied biology, which eventually led to a job in a natural setting—perhaps not a cabin in the woods, but the kind of life that brought fulfillment to his center.

Exercise 7.f – Drawing Your Shadow

The exercise of drawing a shadow part involves a silent dialogue with shadow parts that can be just as revealing as verbal or written methods. As with all the approaches, the more attention you give to a shadow part the less hostile it becomes, and the more information it will give you.

The first drawing (stick figures are fine) should be of the shadow image in whatever way it comes to you, perhaps through a dream, how you fantasize it, an impression that comes with a strong emotion, or the awareness of a secret shame.

For the primitive and the raw, with sexual and hostile images a frequent bill of fare. If your reaction to your boss is seething rage that you've buried, the unconscious can use this opportunity to aim a gun at him.

Remember, this is not about the right or wrong of this energy; it is about the recognition of emotion that has not been acknowledged and the channeling of it in ways that do not harm you or anyone else. By making direct acquaintance with whatever is there, you are establishing an alliance that will provide you with vital information—information you will use to initiate new patterns that will further your ego growth and ultimately empower you in ways never before known.

Exercise 7.g

If you don't have a clear image of the shadow part, you can invite it to make itself known through your feelings or your senses. To do this, make yourself comfortable in a quiet space at a time you will not be disturbed. Close your eyes, take several deep breaths, and let yourself be still for several moments.

Then, think of a situation in which you have identified the presence of the shadow (a projection, an emotional overreaction, a recurring behavior that gets in your way, etc.), and calmly be aware of whatever image comes forward. It could be in the form of a person, it could be a mountain, a rock, or any kind of an object.

The next step (without thinking about the doing of it) is just to let your pen or pencil put to paper what your body-mind connection is manifesting through your hands. Don't be surprised by what you draw. Remember that the unconscious is the repository

Whether drawing the shadow part or communicating with it through written word, you are involved in an organic process with a life and rhythm of its own. You may find yourself drawing or writing to the shadow daily, weekly, or just those times you are aware of its activity. Each encounter strengthens the connection, as the shadow part feels increasingly recognized and taken seriously. No matter what the part says in words or expresses through pictures, you (with the help of your ego-manager mind) are the one responsible for choosing what behaviors will be acted out, not acted out, changed, or left as is. Your conscious mind can even initiate drawings of possible behaviors that allow appropriate expression.

As with the round table technique, the use of the hands in connecting mind and body facilitates a coming together of separated parts (the conscious mind with the unconscious mind). In so doing, new ideas and new ways of being emerge.

Patricia, a woman in her mid-twenties, reported recurring dreams of the stepmother she had during her elementary school years. I suggested she draw a picture of the dream image and bring it to the next session. She returned with two drawings.

The first one was a threatening and surly picture of her stepmother, followed by the image of Patricia pushing her down the stairs. Although embarrassed to show me the second drawing, she knew the implications could not be ignored. Initially shocked by the intensity of what her unconscious was revealing to her, she spent every evening for several weeks letting her hands express her rage through the use of finger paints. Depiction of shaming events generated by her stepmother fueled the painting of red-hot explosions of aggression toward her.

Patricia was not only accessing buried emotion and releasing it in a therapeutic way, over time it led her to examine the effects of her lack of connection with frustration and anger in general. Naming the energy "Red," she eventually related to it as a valued and lovable part of herself, a part that carried previously unknown strength she learned to channel into self- empowering and life-enhancing experiences. The recurring stepmother dream served as the launching pad for soul-searching work and hard-won growth for this young woman.

By the time she brought her therapy to a close, Patricia had expanded from a timid and self-effacing individual to a person in touch with her feelings and self-responsibly pursuing her goals. In regard to her stepmother, her concluding remarks were: "She's no longer in my life, thank heaven, and I know now the frustration I was feeling with anyone who reminded me of her was really tapping into my stuffed anger at her. I have a choice now when I get in touch with that kind of frustration, a choice to remember that this may not be about the person I'm interacting with, but what my unconscious is still dealing with about my stepmother. I can go home and get out the finger paints again."

As Patricia's story shows, and as difficult as it may be, through the process of gradual acquaintance, we learn to connect with shadow energy and to extend longed-for love to rejected parts. Also referred to as infant or child aspects of the self waylaid in their development due to varying kinds of trauma and neglect, their energy is key to the actualization of our wholeness. No matter how despicable a front they may manifest, these disowned segments of our psyches signal and wait for acceptance and integration.

Once again, remember that the journey we take to meet them, to discover who they are behind their menacing masks, and to negotiate meeting their underlying needs can be an intricate and long one. Here our self-nurturing skills are put their keenest test, for the development of trust is essential for these rejected parts to open and receive love. As they feel accepted and nurtured by the more mature features in each of us, their repressed energy transforms. Like ongoing breaths of fresh air, experiences of separation and loneliness are replaced by loving relationships, veins of profound creativity, and the blessing of the Divine within us.

Exercise 7.h

Consider if working with your dreams and daydreams is a likely way for you to work with shadow material. In addition to journal recordings, explore ways you might expand this approach: a dream group, expressing your dream energy through drawings, discussion with a therapist or your support person, etc.

Paradox

Paradox is the label given to any situation in which contradictory and opposing views and behaviors are held and somehow exhibited. We saw how, at the lower stages of ego growth, we think in terms of events, people, and situations as either good or bad. The adage "life should be reasonable and fair" shows its black-and-white strands. Yet over time, edges of experience become fuzzier with previous perceptions of the world becoming harder to confirm. As paradox increasingly creeps in and widens our eyes, the mixing of black and white not only creates gray, but reaches beyond the pale to inclusive shades of all colors and varieties of experience.

Consider the story of Mary and her sister-inlaw, Emma. Having heard from first-hand observers that, in a previous marriage, Emma had physically abused her children, Mary felt scorn for her. She did everything to avoid her presence. As providence would have it, Emma had occasion to appeal to Mary for advice, revealing how depressed she was and the degree to which insomnia was compromising her functioning. On one hand, Mary felt disdain, for she heard nothing from this woman regarding awareness of and responsibility for her past actions, while on the other hand glimmers of compassion stirred as she sensed Emma's pain.

Mary is a self-aware individual, well on her way toward the higher stages of ego growth. Secure in her modest life style and comfortable with her achievements, she devotes considerable attention to the relationship she has with herself and to the world. For some time she's lived in accountable awareness, tracking judgments of others as possible threads to denied parts of her psyche. Yet she was baffled by the contradiction catalyzed by her sister-in-law's revelations. How could she tend to the emotional reaction she had to Emma's past behaviors and how could she foster this newly felt concern?

Such is the riddle of paradox. In snakelike fashion, it winds through life's events, snagging our attention and asking to be resolved. The parent who has long carried bias against the gay community discovers her adored daughter to be a lesbian. The upstanding family man, who once saw himself as a moral pillar of the community, becomes entrenched in a sordid affair. Mothers and fathers vow to be better parents than their own, only to find their children rebelling against their parenting style. Countless situations don't follow logical order or make common sense. One of the most unsettling challenges is that of the mind struggling to understand ambiguity and to make meaning out of seemingly senseless acts— mothers who murder their children, model students who gun down their peers, wealthy CEOs who steal from their employees, and drivers who persist in driving while drunk. Such excruciating and harsh occurrences put us to the ultimate test. So we may appreciate the healthy ego's marvelous capacity for reasoning, organizing, and keeping us on track, awareness of its limitations becomes more real as we approach the higher stages of ego growth.

So what do we do with the irony and contradiction of life events? Dealing with paradox begins with a broadened view of reality. There are two sides to every story, sometimes as many sides as there are listeners and participants.

The worker who regularly criticizes management is in a different position once she is promoted and finds herself supervising employees. Forced to take a second look at previous conceptions, she discovers the how and why of procedures from a different vantage point. On a far-reaching level, the 2001 declaration of "holy war" presents an immensely complicated state of tangled affairs. Beyond what immediately meets the eye is the background of youth recruited for such a mission, evidence indicating that a fair share of these youngsters were separated from their families early in life. Not having had the experience of nurturing attachment in their beginning years and starved for connection and meaning, these impressionable psyches are easily imprinted with hatred, not to mention the notion of supremacy supposedly backed by a sacred cause. On one hand, we are challenged to hold moral awareness of warring actions that are wrong and injurious and even to pursue interventions to halt injustices. On the other hand, we are asked to stretch and consider the consequences of infants and children emotionally blighted for life, no matter where they are found on the globe.

More often than not, paradox includes its own measure of projection. This may or may not be true for Mary, but on deeper exploration it might be found that, somewhere in her background, she behaved in a way that she hasn't yet been able to own. Perhaps she neglected her charges when she was a teenage babysitter, or perhaps she's "forgotten" sexual promiscuity as a young adult that waits for full recognition. Nonetheless, amid her feelings of judgment toward Emma, concern for the woman deepens. "I'm realizing," she said, "that just because I have a negative response to her because of her past behavior, it doesn't rule out caring feelings in the present." Mary has made a huge step toward resolution of this paradoxical situation and all without Emma having any hint of her inner struggle.

Learning to tolerate paradox operates in tandem with the challenges of shadow and projection predicaments. For example, when I recognize my judgment of the slow and inept elderly woman as my own fear of advancing age and begin to deal with this shadow projection, it clears the path to experience her as she is—a woman with her own history of struggles and triumphs. Indeed, the paradox of aging is one of the most difficult to face and eventually emerges for all who live into seniorhood. From the vivacity of youth to the decline of limb and sometimes mind, we must find the strands that hold it all together, going beyond what meets the ordinary eye.

On a larger scale, communities and countries also carry shadow parts fermented with judgment and projection. We participate in collective projection without consciously knowing, due to ways of thinking and acting built into our social fabric. Having grown up in a small town largely populated by descendants of German immigrants, I was aware even in childhood of the value of hard work and the general disregard for those with artistic bent. Musicians, actors, and others who were willing to sacrifice middle class comforts to pursue their goals were considered foolish, if not downright ignorant.

Unfortunately, group projections can be ruthlessly malignant. The "rightness" of religions or the "superiority" of one race over another is played out in conflict after conflict and war after war. In the collective search for targets on which to release venom, judgment unites those who look and act differently—all Muslims become suspected terrorists, Jews greedy, Catholics selfrighteous, and Mexicans lazy. Assumptions are made, blame assigned, with mass consciousness taking over in all-out efforts to root out the enemy. This is how the individual shadow finds safety in numbers and remains in the dark of the collective, the comfort of black/white, good/bad, us/them, always/never keeping us at odds with the total picture and with ourselves.

This is why paradox, projection, and shadow are such major components of the later stages of ego growth. Without their resolution, expansion of the self becomes paralyzed and the stretch into genuine spirituality nullified.

Wondrously, however, with the work of the upper stages of ego growth comes the realization that life is not asking for perfection but unity. Each of us is a mixture of human experiences and human tendencies—the good, the bad, the beautiful, and the ugly. As Carl Jung (1968) so aptly reminded us, both the light and the dark are needed to bring us into wholeness, for without "the suffering of our defects . . . there is no progress and no ascent" (p. 159).

The words of Jungian analyst Jolande Jacobi (1967) underline this in a powerful way when she speaks to the tension between good and evil and the finding of peace only at the center "where man can be wholly man, neither angel nor devil, but simply man, partaker of both worlds . . . the place where the Divine filters through into the soul" (p. 130). The closer we are to the top egogrowth stages, the more astute we become at balancing this teeter-totter. With our feet slightly apart and planted in the middle, the pull from either side—whether "good" from one end or "evil" from the other—requires a shift in weight to hold the center. Without falling to one side or another, without acting out what would be harmful to oneself or another, we accept the reality of what is, make the necessary adjustments, and appreciate the more illumined view.

A core mission of this book involves instilling appreciation that once the threshold of selfawareness is crossed, we each have the capacity to move ever closer to a phenomenal world of expanded inner experience. As the relevance of day-to-day living takes on a different meaning, lessening its dramatic and sometimes melodramatic grip, we have contained within us the power to live from a more consciously aware spiritual paradigm. In so doing, the importance of external accomplishment, accumulation of material goods, and societal approval loosens its primary significance, freeing energy and focus for inner explorations and creative discovery. This does not mean we have a gigantic yard sale or cart truckloads of stuff off to Goodwill, but it does mean that the external world no longer occupies uppermost attention or sponsors ongoing obsessive pursuits.

Instead, we relax into a more natural flow. We enjoy the workings of our thinking mind and understand its limitations. We rely on rational sources of information yet turn to our dreams, fantasies, body knowing, and intuitive inspiration to enrich our endeavors. We see both the relevance of slices of experience along with their fit into the greater whole. We appreciate the thrill of competition while acknowledging its limitations. We give ourselves completely to the moment without being invested in the outcome. We trust the process of creation and dismiss petty concerns. We understand the conventional realm yet welcome the softening line between waking states and other realities. We smell the roses, linger with the sunset, celebrate the joy of a moment, and laugh at our foibles.

Exercise 7.i

◊   What examples of paradox do you have in your present or past history?
◊   How did you deal with these experiences? ◊ Did you find resolution?

to deal with. The shadow is a mastermind of hiding and deception, undermining and derailing us from our paths of integration. Inviting its acquaintance and befriending it takes extreme patience, not unlike dealing with a rebellious teenager who tests us over and over again. "Yes," you say, "I am learning to know and love the vitality of your essence, but your behavior is not acceptable. Whatever it takes and no matter the time involved, you and I will figure out new avenues of expression."

Paradox is much more straightforward. It can hit you broadside or pull the rug out from under your feet. The penchant of paradox for pushing us into acceptance of *what is* cannot be ignored as we sift through the strands of the unfamiliar and the fearful. Partnered with shadow material, the challenge may seem overwhelming. Yet the reward of learning to contain the reality of polar opposites involves the union of all the aspects of who we each are. Delivered from repulsion and darkness, projection, paradox, and all their relations are alchemically transformed into new life energy ready and willing to transcend ego. Know that in your quest of the spiritual and emotional ultimate, you have come a long way. Keep going and allow your wiser self and your intuition to be guides for you—not only as you respond to the exercises but as you prepare to read the descriptions of individual and collective unity in the next chapter.

Last Words

Of all the information in this book, what is put forth in this chapter is probably the most difficult

Exercise 7.j

- ◊ Reread the section beginning on page 110 regarding life asking for unity not perfection. Write a description of an unresolved paradoxical situation in your life.
- ◊ Can you identify the dynamic of projection in this account?
- ◊ Do you detect the hint of shadow material here?
- ◊ What first step can you take to find and maintain a balanced center between the two extremes?

WORKS CITED

Bly, R. (1988). *A little book on the human shadow.* San Francisco: Harper & Row.

Jacobi, J. (1967). *The way of individuation.* (R. F. C. Hull, Trans.). New York: American Library.

Johnson, R. A. (1986). *Inner work: Using dreams and active imagination for personal growth.* San Francisco: Harper & Row.

Jung, C. G. (1968). Psychology and alchemy. (R. F. C. Hull, Trans.) In *The Collected Works*, (12, 2nd ed.), Bollingen Series XX. Princeton, NJ; Princeton University Press.

Miller, W. A. (1991). Finding the shadow in daily life. In C. Zweig & J. Abrams (Eds.), *Meeting the shadow: The hidden power of the dark side of human nature.* Los Angeles: Jeremy Tarcher.

Zweig, C. & Wolf, S. (1997). *Romancing the shadow: Illuminating the dark side of the soul.* New York: Ballentine Books.

DOES DOROTHY GET TO HEAVEN?

While I am not sure if Dorothy in *The Wizard of Oz* had occasional glimpses of the land over the rainbow after she returned home, what she experienced during her journey through Oz stayed with her for life. Similar glimpses of spiritual inspiration fuel many of us. Others adhere to established religious practices to gain reassurance and hope for deliverance from the mundane.

The good news, as these pages will show, is that each of us can uncover the spark that ignites the flame of our innate spirituality. In other words, we don't have to travel to Kansas or Kanpur to find our spiritual pot of gold.

In this chapter, we will follow Dorothy's course through the last stages of ego growth. We will then turn to the writings of Ken Wilber and George Vaillant to see how spirituality threads its way throughout the stages and how the mature ego delivers us into sacred transcendence.

Somewhere Over The Rainbow

In the end of the *Oz* saga, Dorothy's rainbow arced across the sky and touched down on her own Kansas turf. Did Dorothy find her center? Did the sublime eventually saturate her soul? Is that what it means to fly over the rainbow?

As with all of us, no matter where she traveled, Dorothy's psychological package traveled with her. Contained within that parcel was the means for cultivating wholeness, the same no less true for you or me. Dorothy would never tell you her search for the Wizard was a failure. In fact, she told us what she learned: "There's no place like home."

Some of the inherent wisdom of this tale rests in the search for one's place in life and the actualizing of inner potential no matter where we find ourselves. Wherever that may be and in spite of the unpredictable, I once again remind you that the recognition of each situation as an opportunity for learning kindles our growth. We shortchange ourselves in labeling ourselves failures when attempts to master a challenge don't quickly accomplish the ideal or when endeavors seem to work against us, as Dorothy must have initially felt in her discovery of the Wizard behind the veil. Yet this is how the ego goes about its business of making sense of the world—through the juncture of rich, painful, and joyous lessons, it realistically defines itself and moves us further up the growth spiral.

Dorothy's Climb

Let us imagine an adult Dorothy who numbers among the 9 percent of the population who reach for the upper stages of ego growth. I suspect you share something in common with Dorothy—pursuit of the ultimate only to return to your homeland with a more reflective point of view. So, no matter where you have ventured in the past or where you find yourself stationed in the present, let this mythical narrative deepen your imprint of emotional and spiritual integration, once again guided by Loevinger's and Cook-Greuter's data (as presented in chapter 3).

Tuning in to a middle-aged Dorothy positioned at the individualistic eighth stage, no longer looking "out there" for enlightened answers, we find an astute individual who experiences herself as a unique human being, depending on her own insight and ingenuity to weave possibility and practicality into reality. Excelling as a career biologist after graduating from college, Dorothy's work as a cancer research specialist corresponds with her belief in the capacity of science to heal humankind's dilemmas. Though she lives alone, spending time with friends brings her pleasure, while traveling satisfies her sense of adventure and penchant to experience the unknown.

Dorothy was in her mid-twenties when she attained the sixth ego-growth stage, and with self-help information and a journal for recording insights, she effectively identified and related to many of her feelings and learned to be more assertive in the work place. However, she neglected to probe deeper and did not dare to share new perceptions with others, so the acute loneliness that permeates her midlife transition, with its agonizing emotional isolation, comes as a total shock to her.

By a stroke of good fortune, Dorothy joins a midlife support group that catalyzes an in-depth review of what life has or has not provided her. She, the responsible one, the creator of her destiny, has to find out what is missing.

What has she not gained? What has she lost? True, her feeling of youth is beginning to fade, but what she discovers at the core is how she has never cultivated intimate relationships. The family and friends of her youth are neither geographically or emotionally close (faulty infant attachment no doubt a factor). She has felt no need for the confidence of a "best friend," and most baffling in this appraisal has been her lack of interest in men. Self-pleasuring is no stranger to her, as she takes care of her own needs. Yet here is Dorothy's shadow leering over her shoulder as she sits in the support group and hears feedback regarding how emotionally distant she seems to them.

Dorothy slinks home with mixed feelings of resentment and relief, later writing in her journal: "I feel terror when I think of exposing myself. I feel repulsed when others so openly 'emote'— completely disgusted by those who effortlessly seem to do what I don't choose or have enough guts to do."

She puts it one way. I put it another: shadow is doing its work, and the group feedback vis-àvis the third Johari pane (what others see in me that I don't see in myself (as presented in chapter 7)), opens the window to this projection.

The flow gradually swells between what was hidden and is now within clear view, as journal entries give words to repressed energy crying out for human closeness and especially with a man!

In spite of overwhelming terror of rejection, Dorothy musters courage to share her discoveries with the group, a group that in no way abandons her. With gentle and loving acceptance, they support her throughout weeks of emotional exposure—including expressions of grief for early life attachment deficiencies. Dorothy becomes the winner of "earned security" as she internalizes this holding environment and the art of selflove. Along with this, she develops the capacity to choose discriminately when, how, and with whom to share her emotional realities.

Ready for the next step, Dorothy yields to the inevitable and starts to date. When she falls in love with a man and they ease into to a live-in relationship, the delight of a whole new way of life, including sustained sexual intimacy, totally enthralls her. However, as time passes, conflict between what her partner has become used to— the mesmerized exclusivity of the early months of their relationship—and continues to expect begins to compromise her functioning in the workplace. His complaint that she spends too much time at work and visiting with friends on days off greatly annoys her—successful completion of a challenging project would most likely result in a long-sought career promotion and having time with friends in the long run is very important to her. How to handle the struggle between emotional dependency and self-sufficiency? From Dorothy's perspective, this conflict both comes from within herself and from outside herself. It isn't just her dissatisfaction, it's his behavior as well. Dorothy loves this man and does not want to part ways, while a secret part of her yearns for the days when she lived alone and was totally self-reliant—a prime example of initiation into the paradox of relationship. When she suggests counseling, he is quick to decline, amplifying the intensity of their struggle. Knowing she must develop more elasticity in the "how to" of emotional intimacy, she once again turns to selfhelp books. Fortified with information as to how to improve communication, she then institutes an improved style of relating her emotional plight to him. Over a period of months, encouraging shifts occur in both expectations and behaviors. This helps Dorothy see how relative everything is—feelings may be one way one day and surface quite differently the next. Experiencing how context and points of view are central to understanding, Dorothy develops more compassion for her partner's selfhood and more tolerance for their differences. In addition, she becomes quite adept at choosing times she is willing to "give in" to togetherness and those times when she opts to be alone. Other times, she chooses to engage in negotiation with the goal of a win-win situation.

In the successful navigation of the eighth individualistic stage, Dorothy does not desert her core self but courageously applies her ingenuity to create a life resilient enough to dance between emotional dependence and independence. That her shadow energy does not catch up to her until this stage exemplifies the unevenness of growth, for as previous examples have shown, initial awareness of what is projected or hidden often emerges during stages six and seven. However, the unsparing reality she encountered during the eighth stage not only heals her emotional dearth but also brings her moments of spiritual insights far beyond the conscientious and responsible levels. With the internalization of a holding environment, she both integrates repressed energy and progresses into the joy of self-love and the love of others—an impressive triumph over the complexity of what turned out to be a very transitional phase in Dorothy's spiral through the stages.

Movement into the ninth ego-growth stage of autonomy presents a more natural fit, its challenges resonating more with Dorothy's youthful pursuits and her ongoing romance with expanding inner and outer horizons. The seasoned relationship with her partner allows more flexibility, and Dorothy sets out *to be the most she can be*, eager to learn more about life, about her potential, and about how higher development is closer to the truth. Thus, from her self-generated core identity and with appreciation of her uniqueness as master of her destiny, Dorothy intensifies commitment to ongoing self- development. Holding on to the insights of her midlife transition, she knows there are no simple answers. She, like all others, is a revolving and evolving emotional and spiritual being, ascending her growth spiral from constantly shifting perspectives.

A. Lack of assertiveness
B. Emotional detachment
C. Need to develop capacity to self-soothe
D. Grief regarding early life faulty attachment
E. Lack of intimate relationships

So what does this Dorothy do? This Dorothy who wants to taste, to touch, to see, to hear, to feel all that she can gives heed to her intuition. The world she has known, this technologically shrinking, environmentally-threatened planet, is being pulled at the seams by hunger, poverty, and social injustice that she can no longer ignore. At the same time, she deeply desires to continue nourishing her carefully cultivated relationship with her mate, as well as ties with close friends. Ready to simplify her life style and liberate her intense job attachment, she chooses to work halftime. Although her partner does not share her social zeal, he respects her immersion in collective undertakings and is grateful for her devotion to their relationship. Hence, she furthers her self-actualization by reading cross-cultural literature, observing activist gatherings, and by viewing foreign documentaries. Both self-empowered and vulnerable, the more she learns the more she recognizes similarities between herself and all others, no matter the culture or geography. The naiveté of her childhood foray is now replaced by valuable experiences of complexities and polarities, as Dorothy is grounded in a worldwide, here-and-now reality.

Especially interested in healthcare, Dorothy volunteers at a local community health center. Eventually, her passage through the autonomous stage culminates in traveling as a volunteer with an organization providing healthcare to third-world countries.

On the completion of her mission, Dorothy returns home in a very reflective state of mind. While on one hand she found volunteer experiences to be very fulfilling, on the other hand the possibility that her thoughts, her emotions, and her actions cannot alone provide what she is looking for distresses her.

What has happened is that the first part of the tenth stage—that of construct aware—is now transparent. Consequently, Dorothy's focus shifts from being the most she can be *to being aware*. Conventional ways of thinking are no longer of interest. She wants to know, amid all her complexity, the processes and imprints that exist in her brain and scrutinize them as closely as she can.

At the same time, her external world presents its own demands. Her partner, now retired and struggling with multiple health problems, is in need of her assistance. Sorrowed by his condition and treasuring the days he has left, Dorothy copes by retiring from her job to provide for his needs. As she spends time with him, she also observes the boundaries of her mind. She reaps benefits from this dual capacity of experiencing the hereand-now while cultivating expanded spiritual insights that provide glimpses into other planes of reality. When her partner nears death, something opens within him. The sharing of his feelings— the resistance, the fear, the anger, and eventually the acceptance—endows Dorothy with a sense of transcendence. Holding his hand throughout his final transition, she gives in to the awareness that something other than the mind—a consciousness beyond reason, analysis, and the personal—is involved. Peace breathes into her heart as her beloved draws his last breath.

Nonetheless, as a sensate and caring individual, she finds grief has no mercy. For some months she gives in to the anguish of the loss, with full appreciation of the fundamental magnitude of honest emotional expression.

At the same time, she remembers and revisits the deeper connectedness that pervaded the last days with her mate. As a result, she begins to entertain unitary concepts and to think beyond culture and beyond her own lifetime. Her view of humans as beings much invested in intellectual pursuits fades, and her sense of self as a permanent object lessens. She begins to see through the illusion of individuals as stable and independent entities and beholds a vast interrelated mass of human dysfunction— the colliding reality of limitations and challenges faced by all individuals, communities, and nations at large. While at times feelings of nothingness overwhelm her, Dorothy also holds the tension of existential paradox and understands the ways in which we are separated from truth. Parallel to this, she treasures the depth and breadth of the threading of generations throughout life as she interacts with her friend's great-grandchildren. More and more she thinks beyond perceived reality. Her ego has accumulated enough history to know itself as a bounded, essential point of reference. Now, as Dorothy sees her relative insignificance in the totality of human existence, she longs to transcend conscious ego.

Finally Dorothy reaches the tenth stage—the stage of *to be*, of ultimate integration, with its profound new way of perceiving existence and consciousness. Also called the universal or unitive stage, she develops global vision, described by Cook-Greuter (1990) as a new paradigm in which an individual such as Dorothy:

> . . . sees and experiences [herself] and others as part of ongoing humanity, embedded in the process of creation. The two sides of Pascalian paradox are now integrated. Feelings of belongingness and feelings of one's own separateness and uniqueness are experienced without undue tension.

Integrated persons have the ability to look at themselves and at others in terms of the passing of ages, of near and far in geographical, social, cultural, historical, intellectual, and developmental dimensions. They can take multiple points of view and shift focus instantly and effortlessly. They feel embedded in nature: birth, growth, and death, joy and pain, are seen as natural occurrences, as patterns of change in the flux of time. Rational, waking consciousness is no longer perceived as a shackle but as just another phenomenon that assumes foreground or background status depending on the momentary focus (p. 93).

So it is with an integrated Dorothy. She can grasp truth, but she realizes her mind can never conquer it. She accepts herself as she is, no longer trying to control people, circumstances, or events. Instead she channels her energy into a myriad of creative pursuits, including embracing her growing need to transcend the limitations of her ego. Here at the pinnacle of ego growth, Cook-Greuter (1990) tells us, "Other realities, such as altered states, become increasingly important, worthy of exploration, and crucial for deeper understanding, with previous out-of-this-world peak experiences developing into ongoing natural occurrences" (p. 93).

Dorothy explores the transcendent through meditation and through her own kind of prayer. Spending a great deal of time alone in nature, she spontaneously drifts into states of consciousness wherein the fading of individuality is overtaken by a sense of sacred connection. In her discovery of how feelings of gratitude amplify experience, she wakes in the night transported into the beyond. In finding her way completely home into wholeness, Dorothy now uses her ego as an anchor for spiritual expansion and encountering of the Divine within her—the wisdom of the Wizard finally unveiling itself.

Exercise 8.a

Reread the above description of the characteristics of an integrated person. List any you have either attained or made progress toward attaining. Then list the one you think would be the hardest to achieve. Write about the relationship this characteristic has to the issues on your ego-growth spiral and to your current ego-growth stage.

What Ken Wilber Has To Say

Ego researchers bring us to a certain point in their conclusions, including the ways in which the spiritual qualities of empathy and altruism manifest the mature ego. Without going into detail, they tease us with the possibility of numinous awakening and an embedded Zen-like acceptance of life. For some, this seems a sterile option. For many, it increasingly becomes a worthy goal as the emptiness of endless acquisition seeps through the cracks of Western civilization, begging for moral, social, and political repair. Through it all, across centuries of time and multitudes of religious approaches, the fundamental message is the same: love and compassion shape the heart of mystical attunement and underlie the thrust of true spiritual connection.

Unfortunately, religions tend to fixate on doctrine, splitting hairs over tradition and beliefs, losing sight of their missions. Over and over again, we miss this glue that binds our brotherhood. Fearful of losing our uniqueness, we have yet to learn that coats of many colors can gather at the table of togetherness without losing their hue and that individuality can flourish in a respectful stream of humanity. We can hope that not too far in the distant future as more and more of us reach the pinnacle of maturity, our spirits will be freed to altruistically soar.

But what do these words really mean? Shouldn't the ego just melt away in the heat of spiritual enlightenment? Ken Wilber (1998a), for one, doesn't think so. This genius philosopher has written volumes about the plight of the human condition in relation to spiritual advancement.

As we saw in chapter 3, the word *spiritual* pertains to the spirit or soul as distinguished from physical nature. Religion, on the other hand, involves a set of beliefs concerning the cause, nature, and purpose of the universe, usually involving devotional and ritual observances, and often containing a moral code. Obviously, the word *spiritual* is a looser term, not restricted by practices of an institution or adherence to a doctrine. In a spiritual and holistic universe, the soul is touched by everything, and its growth enhanced by the way in which we respond to the experiences and challenges encountered along the way. The paradox is that while an individual who is involved in religion can indeed be spiritual, there are many individuals so caught up in the physical form of religion they give little or no attention to the soul or the spirit. Consequently, those who engage in religious tradition out of habit or who are trapped by fear of the unknown may stall in the conformist stage.

Their inability to grasp a broader understanding of the true essence of the soul impedes growth momentum toward higher stages.

From a much broader perspective, Wilber (1998a) draws on the "perennial philosophy" found at the core of the world's great traditions— from Christianity to Taoism and all that is in between. Central to this philosophy is belief in the idea of the "Great Chain of Being," a continuum of reality extending in hierarchical order from matter to body to mind to soul to spirit. Wilber says, ". . . men and women can grow and develop (or evolve) all the way up the hierarchy to Spirit itself" (p. 39).

This dynamite spiritual talk speaks to every human being's right to mystical aspiration and the inborn potential to attain it. Encompassing all of life, this evolution unfolds through increasing orders of wholeness. In the physical domain, cells divide and form organs; organs join to make up systems of the body. In the mental domain, a youngster first learns to count and later to incorporate these basic numbers into complicated equations. In the psychological domain, a kindergartner may punch his classmate to protect his territory, when years later he approaches his adversary with calm and reason. In the spiritual domain, we may initially do good works to avoid the wrath of a punishing God, and then gradually expand into the experience of giving without need for reward.

As we have already seen, such is the nature of how we grow and develop—the limited and seemingly small functions we come into this world with are added to by increasingly complex patterns and capacities, each stage expanding our unity and broadening our identity as well. We move forward from the symbiotic connection of infancy through separation and individuation to ultimate integration, while surpassing and including all that went before. So, as you move to the eighth stage of ego growth, you are transcending the seventh while incorporating the teachings of the seventh and all the preceding stages. Stalling, failure, and even fragmentation at any given stage notwithstanding, our inborn potential is meant to spiral.

Wilber takes the ego researchers' work an octave higher when he refers to the process involved in the negotiation of ever-ascending levels of consciousness. Speaking to this holistic hierarchy in which networks of human growth unfold in stages, with each higher dimension more inclusive and closer to the Godhead, Wilber (1998a) states: "Spirit is the summit of being, the highest rung on the ladder of evolution. But it is also true that Spirit is *the wood out of which the entire ladder and all its rungs are made.*

Spirit is the suchness, the isness, the essence of each and everything that exists" (p. 44). In short, spirituality is at the core of all expressions of life.

While much of the foregoing entails spiritual perceptions (in contrast to scientific validation), this theorist's recognition of developmental stages is indeed relevant. Specifically drawing on Loevinger's model, Wilber (1998a) concludes, "The ego as a competency is maintained in higher development, but the ego as an exclusive sense of identity is replaced by higher and wider identities" (pp. 149-150). What he means is that the self-capacity developed by the ego to deal with the material world remains intact to keep us alive, connected, and hopefully in good health. We eat, tend to our bodies, have relationships with others, and look out for the safety of ourselves. At the same time, the highly developed ego becomes less and less bound by individual identification and actually anchors its capacity to be effectively in the world while expanding the sense of self from the individual "I" stationed at the center of the world to the more collective "I" in relation to the world. Simply put, the ego does not go away as we evolve. From the first stage to the last and beyond, we are immersed in a spiritual world and engaged in spiritual work.

All this paints a neat picture on paper. The fact of the matter is the doing of it is actually quite messy. Wilber (1998a) minces no words when he describes our arrival into a world fraught with separation and alienation, wherein we move "from unconscious Hell to *conscious* Hell" (p. 53). The oneness many believe we all are born with—the ground of our being in union with the Divine—is lost to conscious awareness. As our journey unfolds, we are dizzied by the rudeness of life and spend years trying to right the matter. We think the answer rests in making the outside world accountable and fair, setting out to conquer forces that stand in our way. We may even make headway in the first half of our lives—the right job, the right spouse, planned arrival of children, and so on. Yet something inside us whispers of lack, of unfulfilled connection, and the knowing of how, in the end, mortality will have its way.

About this time we are most likely due for that shift midway through the ego-growth stages. Perhaps someone close to us dies, one of our children fails in a big way, we develop a life-threatening illness, or a world crisis erupts.

Conscious hell breaks loose as it becomes impossible to ignore the pain and struggle. Slowly the realization dawns that things will never be the same and that what is broken cannot be fixed. It is a critical crossroads, for we can either blame fate while frantically expressing our frustration and anger or face the truth of what is.

This is not to recommend the repression of emotion. As we have seen, shock, anger, and overwhelming grief are part of our emotional repertoire so that, when devastating and hurtful events occur, their appropriate flow is essential for the healing. The hazard is becoming stuck in an emotional response that doubles back on itself, creating a repetitive loop with no exit. The individual sexually abused in childhood who decades later is still consumed by feelings of hatred toward the perpetrator has yet to reach the realization: "I may not have been able to prevent what happened to me, but I can work with the response I have and move beyond this crippling stage of my life."

Sadly for some, being conscious of the hell they are experiencing does become a fixed part of life. Suspended on one of the lower stages of ego growth, they dare not shift their weight for fear of losing foothold and falling into an ever-burning inferno. Such blockage can braid into bitterness and cynicism, complicated by obstinate depression or obsessive need for revenge. Such great wounding calls for defenses equal to the task, requiring extraordinary healing circumstances to mend.

Moving from "unconscious hell to conscious hell" means many things and in no way implies a lack of capacity for movement beyond. The hell part means we cannot control the outside world. We know the conscious part means we take seriously our responses to the vicissitudes of life. We surrender to external reality but also take on the mantle of the spiritual warrior who knows the bottom-line battle is with the self, specifically so in regard to how we react to the difficult situations in which we find ourselves. Through expanded awareness and the acceptance of inner responsibility, the maturing ego promotes spiritual maturity, for in order to spiritually mature, we must have a mature ego. With the melding of ego and spiritual maturity, we transcend the sense of a separate self and move closer to conscious heaven, where eventually, according to Wilber (1998b), we experience complete union—the realization of our "Supreme Identity with Spirit itself" (p. 97).

Exercise 8.b

- ◊ How would you describe the existence of spirituality in your life right now?
- ◊ How has religion (or a religious institution) impacted your life?

Exercise 8.c

Given what Ken Wilber says about spirituality, describe in writing the spiritual thread that has woven and continues to weave through your life.

Exercise 8.d

Describe a time in your life when you were in unconscious hell. Describe a time when you were in conscious hell. What role did spirituality play in these two experiences?

What George Vaillant Has To Say

Once again, we meet up with psychiatrist George Vaillant, whom we have met in previous chapters. We know his research showed that defense mechanisms are real and can be measured. He also demonstrated how ego maturity is very much dependent on the capacity to soothe oneself. In addition, greatly influenced by the observation of research subjects whose egos had matured, Vaillant (1993) described their spirituality in terms of "religious wonder":

> Mature defenses grow out of our brain's capacity to master, assimilate, and feel gratitude for life, living, and experience. Such gratitude encompasses the capacity for wonder. To see and comprehend the joy of a sunset or a symphony or to sustain a mature religious conviction is evidence that one's mind has experienced a hallucination or an illusion of sorts. Such wonder is in itself a transformation and a self-deception of the most sublime nature (p. 337).

Further consideration of this phenomenon led Vaillant (1993) to attribute spiritual development to four components: the dreaming we do both at night and during the day; the seeking out of sacred places; the capacity to play; and the integration of emotion and thought. The first three components involve imagination and augment the love we have already internalized. Integration of emotion and thought produce mature defense mechanisms. Taken all together, the four components "help to foster the spiritual and psychological growth that sometimes allows us to develop hope, faith, and gratitude" (p. 338).

As a result of the foregoing, Vaillant spent a number of years studying the relationship between mammalian evolution and human spirituality. In his 2008 book, *Spiritual Evolution: A Scientific Defense of Faith*, he presents evidence that spirituality originates in the limbic system, that it reflects humankind's need for connection, and that our brains are hardwired for the expression of positive emotions.

From chapter 6, you already know that the limbic system is the seat of emotions in the brain, with the flow of neuropeptides carrying emotional information throughout the entire body. Vaillant shows how the limbic brain, in its mediation of emotions and interaction with the frontal brain (neocortex), provides the capacity for human connection and is essential to survival. The quality of this limbic dynamic dates back to the manner in which parents emotionally interact with their offspring: parents who show love and acceptance of infants through eye contact, touch, and responsiveness to their needs instill trust in their progeny.

In contrast, recall the research from chapter 2 in which Dr. Renee Spitz filmed infants who were hospitalized for an extended time and how they eventually withdrew into cocoons of emotional despair and hopelessness. Since their limbic brains were not connecting to their frontal brains and they did not experience human connection, their physical survival was at stake.

Vaillant (2008) affirms how the emergence of newer sciences (neuroscience, cultural anthropology, and ethology) has demonstrated the "subcortical, limbic, mammalian capacity for positive emotion and for altruistic action" (p. 20). Even though Candace Pert describes all emotions as positive because they provide information to support our survival, Vaillant makes a distinction regarding positive ones in relation to spirituality. Vaillant's list includes the following:

- ◊ Faith
- ◊ Love
- ◊ Hope
- ◊ Joy
- ◊ Forgiveness
- ◊ Compassion
- ◊ Awe
- ◊ Mystical illumination

Obviously, this capacity for positive emotion depends on a ripened ego with the use of mature defense mechanisms.

Citing rituals and cultural formats of great religions as the surest way to bring positive emotions into conscious awareness, Vaillant (2008) states, "Neuroscience, like cultural anthropology, has affirmed the relevance of religious ritual to connect with the limbic world of emotion" (p. 191).

Furthermore, he describes how the technology of brain imaging shows that intense meditation allows us to "attend to the reality of the inner, more 'spiritual' world." While not advocating strict adherence to religious beliefs, Vaillant places great value on scientifically substantiated practices that expand love for self and others, instill respect for religious institutions, and further evolutionary advance. While both Vaillant and Wilber include Loevinger's ten ego-growth stages in their conclusions, Vaillant strengthens his perspective with the addition of the significance of the ability to nurture and soothe one's self.

Exercise 8.e

Write down three experiences that have most influenced your spiritual perspective and note what they have in common. Review the section on paradox in chapter 7, and examine the role of paradox in these experiences. Explore how these experiences can help you to resolve paradox in your life today and to expand your spirituality.

Summary

In this chapter, you have explored the terrain of ego-growth stages eight, nine, and ten, via Dorothy's simulated venture. Are you inspired by the profile of an integrated individual who reaches the pinnacle? Ken Wilber and George Vaillant, each of whom base spiritual transcendence on a mature ego, were turned to for insights and conclusions regarding the spiritual evolution of humankind.

In the next and final chapter, you will learn research results about those who reach the top stages of ego growth, with corresponding implications both for you as an individual and for humanity as a whole.

WORKS CITED

Cook-Greuter, S. R. (1990). Maps for living: Ego development stages from symbiosis to conscious universal embeddedness. In M. Commons, C. Armon, et al. (Eds.), *Adult development: Vol. 2, Models and methods in the study of adolescent and adult thought*study of adolescent and adult thought 103). New York: Praeger.

Loevinger, J. & Wessler, R. (1970). *Measuring ego development: Vol. 1. Construction and use of a sentence completion test.* San Francisco: Jossey-Bass.

Vaillant, G. E. (1993). *The wisdom of the ego.* Cambridge, MA: Harvard University Press. Vaillant, G. E. (2008). *Spiritual evolution: A scientific defense of faith.* New York: Broadway Books.

Wilber, K. (1998a). *The eye of spirit: An integral vision for a world gone slightly mad.* Boston: Shambhala.

Wilber, K. (1998b). *The essential Ken Wilber: An introductory reader.* Boston: Shambhala.

Amazing Grace:
Scientific Convergence and Beyond

Endings are also beginnings. Eight chapters ago marked your initiation into a new way of thinking about and acting on personal growth. Reading this last chapter brings to closure an official overture to the mature ego, though the refrain of the previous chapters will carry you forward and beyond this book.

In this final chapter, you will examine how the tenth and final stage of ego growth forms a scientifically proven base for expansion of consciousness with fine-tuned glimpses of what lies beyond.

You will learn how the concept of self-actualization dovetails with ego maturity and how results from diverse researchers impart similar portrayals of such maturity. You will be buoyed by what this ultimate development means for you as an individual and what it means for the planet as a whole. And as you turn the last page, the imprint of holistic potential will serve as your own reminder of how you are meant to grow and who your deeper self knows you to be.

Self-Actualization

What is self-actualization? Is it a stand-alone event? Does reaching the top ego-growth stage mean living in a vacuum, with intimate relationships falling to the wayside? Far to the contrary, according to Abraham Maslow (1970), the 1950s leader of the humanistic psychology movement. Describing "self- actualized" individuals as those *who live their potential to the fullest*, Maslow's research enlarged the picture of an integrated being. Known for his hierarchy of needs, Maslow used a broad-based pyramid to illustrate his stepped theory of growth. According to this model and in ascending order, we fulfill our needs beginning with basic physical needs (food and shelter), followed by safety needs (security and freedom from fear), psychology needs (belonging, love, acceptance, and self-esteem), and at the very top, fulfillment of one's far reaching potential and self-actualization. Maslow concluded from his studies that self-actualization was probably not possible until we number among the senior crowd—a conclusion most likely congruent with the spiritual and social profile of the time.

Maslow's research (1970) included digging into history books for evidence of individuals who fully lived their potential, identifying both Thomas Jefferson and Abraham Lincoln (in his later years) as self-actualized people. He also considered Albert Einstein, Eleanor Roosevelt, Jane Addams, William James, Albert Schweitzer, Aldous Huxley, and Benedict de Spinoza as very probable candidates. While he found these individuals carried an air of detachment and a need for privacy, they also displayed a fresh appreciation for people and life, deeply identifying with humankind.

Self-actualizers have profound and deeply emotional intimate relationships with a few close people and demonstrate democratic values and attitudes. They do not confuse means with end and exercise a philosophical sense of humor lacking in hostility. They tap into a wellspring of creativity.

Furthermore, Maslow found that self-actualized individuals are realistically oriented and accepting of themselves, others, and the world. They are spontaneous, autonomous, independent, and problem-centered in contrast to self-centered (Maslow, 1970). According to researchers Hall and Lindzey (1978) self-actualizers do not conform to culture and "transcend the environment rather than just coping with it" (p. 270). In regard to spiritual orientation these researchers state, "Most self-actualized persons have had profound mystical or spiritual experiences, although not necessarily religious in character" (p. 269).

Unitive Equals Integrative

The foregoing describes a blend of realism and transcendence that Maslow (1971) refers to as *unitive*. This unitive way of being parallels the integrative stage of the pinnacle stage of ego growth. Claiming that only 1 percent of the population reach this ultimate, he coined the term "being psychology" (in contrast to doing), writing in detail about the world we experience once this state of unitive beingness is reached. The similarity between his portrayal of self-actualized individuals and descriptions of ego maturity put forth by the ego researchers is striking. Across the board, Abraham Maslow, George Vaillant, Jane Loevinger, and Suzanne Cook-Greuter agree that these individuals:

- View occurrences of life in relative terms
- Have integrative experiences of unity
- Demonstrate altruistic behaviors
- Take pleasure in intimate relationships
- Carry the capacity for total attention to tasks
- Understand the irrelevance of comparison and competition
- Experience a disappearance of self when absorbed in experience
- Accept reality as it is
- Recognize limitations of the mind
- Experience resolution of paradox
- Show humor and playfulness
- Pursue creative expression
- Hold a sense of awe
- Have familiarity with peak experiences

Everything on this list is familiar to you. We have seen each of these items presented in one form or another in our study of the escalating stages of ego growth as well as in the description of the mature defense mechanisms. What we have here are concrete descriptions from a number of sound investigators, illustrating in unison what it means to have a grown-up ego.

Exercise 9.a

Copy this list into your journal. Picture yourself manifesting all of these characteristics. Put a star μ next to the ones you have actually experienced (whether briefly or long-term).

Make another list of those you have not experienced and those you have experienced. Label this list: "What I am growing toward." Put this on your mirror or refrigerator—and remember never to call it quits!

Think of what it would mean for *you* to live in awe of life; to be able to give your total attention to whatever you are doing; to be in the moment, whether it is a conversation with a loved one or sitting at the side of the river, absorbed in its flow; to accept events and people as they are, with no inner banter of judgment or expectation; to not care what your neighbors think; to feel unity within yourself and unity with others, without attaching importance to competition and comparison; to have peak experiences that take you beyond time and space; to appreciate your rational mind while being aware of its limits and trappings; to daily exhibit spontaneity and enjoy the many ways you have learned to play; to manifest healthy humor; to be able to hold in calm acceptance the challenge of paradox and the relative nature of occurrences; and to let your creative juices flow.

While it may be disconcerting to read Maslow's claim of only 1 percent reaching the very top, this is neither substantiated by firm research nor reflective of a twenty-first-century statement. If present day sales of self-help books and the number of people seeking therapy for holistic reasons mean anything, the percentage of those crossing the threshold into self-awareness is on an inspiring rise and is certainly not reserved just to the senior population. This, in part, may be related to baby boomers faced with the middle-aged question of what brings deeper purpose and meaning to their lives.

Just as much to the point is how, in the evolutionary scheme of things, the front "thinking" part of the brain continues to increase in size, not to mention the brain's capacity to produce neurons that replace dysfunctional ones. This suggests that the fortunate individuals dedicated to growth endeavors are working appropriately within their reach. In short, it appears the top half of the stages may well be sprouting with those committed to conscientious living.

Vaillant Revisited

Vaillant's (1993) research brings forward another encouraging aspect of this upper terrain. Notably, many of his subjects were ordinary people appearing to lead ordinary lives, with a segment of the sample coming from very disadvantaged childhoods, both environmentally and emotionally. Upon close examination of eleven subjects from such backgrounds, Vaillant discovered after fifty years of follow-up that eight showed relatively mature ego defenses. These individuals were able to laugh at themselves, they showed empathy, they knew how to plan realistically, and they kept a stiff upper lip as situations called for—in other words, they exhibited the mature defenses of humor, altruism, anticipation, suppression, and sublimation. Such resilient individuals remind us all that the capacity for hanging out on the top stages of ego growth does not necessarily depend on a secure and comfortable early environment. And once again, it is a reminder that it is never too late to grow up the self.

Peak Experience And Beyond

According to Maslow (1970), total absorption in any occurrence, whether internal or external, may lead to a peak experience, leading him to define it in this way:

> The acute mystic or peak experience is a tremendous intensification of *any* of the experiences in which there is loss of self or transcendence of it, such as problem centering, intense concentration, . . . intense sensuous experience, self-forgetful and intense enjoyment of music or art (p. 165).

In this description, an altered state of consciousness (ASC) to the exclusion of everything else is taken to an elevated level. Art, poetry, nature, beauty, and sensual and sexual experiences that overwhelm cause us to lose track of time and space and serve as entry ways into a realm beyond our finite selves. Equally significant is the realization that something valuable has happened, so the person in some way is strengthened and transformed.

Numerous times, clients have related such phenomena to me—attending a loved one at the time of death; witnessing the birth of a child; winning a race; reaching the summit of a mountain; finding a long-lost relative; having a near-death experience—pinnacle events that spawn more fulfilling directions in lives and propel movement toward growth. From a peak experience perspective, the individual in such a state feels unified. For the time being, the internal tug of war between opposite polarities is transcended with openness and spontaneity fully in evidence.

While peak experiences are possible at any stage of development, they are reported more frequently by those very close to or at the top of the growth spectrum. The unitive stage at the apex *is* profoundly spiritual, wherein individuals express the desire to move even beyond self-actualization towards self-transcendence and deeper wisdom.

Creativity

Once our energy is no longer bound up in keeping the inner hound—our shadow self—at bay, it is freed for manifestations emanating from the true self. No longer fearing our inner impulses, no longer fixated on performance and achievement, our boundaries become more permeable. We open to transpersonal influences wherein access to unseen energies—a "felt" contact with something outside ourselves—enlightens our expression. Such creativity emerging from a typical state of consciousness is said to be numinous, that is, it connects us with the Divine. Curiously enough, according to psychologist Joel Funk (2000), geniuses who have not yet reached the unitive stage are said to have the ability to access this transcendent consciousness, at least some of the time.

Inspired creativity involves an openness described as "active passivity." While the individual is indeed occupied with the labor of what is being created, he feels essentially passive, as though the creation is generating itself. In such instances, the person who is serving as a vehicle for the flow will say things like: "It just came through me," or "All I did was sit here and let it happen." At the same time, ego capacities remain intact as the individual goes about organizing and managing the input into a synthesized whole.

By our willingness to be open to what comes through our senses, we welcome the boldness, immediacy, and clarity that underscore invention. Resonating to something greater and more intelligent, we allow ourselves to be vehicles of discovery, innovators of the new, and manifesters of the sacred. The muse infused by the numinous carries the capacity to transform—that is, this creative energy becomes alchemical, purifying our intentions and spinning the energy of emotional straw into spiritual gold. We may create a celebratory ritual, be inspired by the vision of a holy shrine, carve out a new kind of physical space, or swim in the gaze of our beloved with fresh, open eyes. We enrich ourselves and the communities in which we live by contributions that are unsullied by avarice and personal gain.

The Beyond

While theorists and metaphysicians, including Ken Wilber, offer outlines mapping higher consciousness terrain, the endpoint of *Grow Up Your Ego* is to assure readers of the evidence that integrative consciousness can be obtained—and when it is, a threshold is crossed into a transcendent and open-ended domain. Within this domain, the experience of "a self" (the ego) supports the experience of "no self" (beyond the ego), with exploration of what lies within the within (Wilber, 1998b). This, it has been said, is the call of the soul back to itself, wherein an observing part of our being increasingly applies itself. Another way of describing this experience of "a self" supporting the experience of "no self" is this: the ego in its maturity has enough strength to support the opening that allows the flow of Divine light through the self which is the light and power of the soul.

No matter how hierarchies of higher consciousness may be described by religions and metaphysical philosophies, all culminate in union with the Soul—the Absolute, the Divine, the Self, or whatever term is yours. From this union ensues a sense of ultimate belonging. The individual who has reached the unitive stage naturally feels drawn toward mystical union. For it is agreed that efforts such as meditation, prayer, ritual, and related practices are generally required to strengthen the witnessing mind for union and enlightenment to occur. Whatever means are used to further expansion of consciousness and whatever discipline is followed, individuals who are navigating in the beyond increasingly commit themselves to spiritual pursuits. While their egos continue to organize and manage their lives, their hearts and souls seek out pathways enhancing Divine union.

Evolution Is Upon Us

One hundred years ago, grade-school children knew little more than what they read in textbooks of other cultures and had no notion of global dilemmas. Religious institutions remained unto themselves, the thought of ecumenical exchange heretical. Now the word *spiritual* slips into daily jargon, often replacing the word *religion*. The spiritual thread Vaillant found weaving through many of his subjects' lives did not necessarily refer to church-going activities but to the ability to transcend ordinary reality and to experience what is beyond. And as you so well know, such movement toward the spiritual naturally occurs as the ego matures.

No longer able to ignore this accelerating shift, we see the effects falling into place all around us. Clearly, increase in the size of the human brain across the evolutionary span accounts for greater intelligence, with sophisticated brain imaging showing how specific areas of the brain light up during meditation and prayer. Equally relevant is that many scholars have long believed that expanded consciousness—illumined perception and spiritual experience outside the linear mind—is integral to this unfolding. Teilhard de Chardin (1959), the French Jesuit paleontologist who was as much mystic as scientist, alleged that, since the beginning of time, the edge of evolution has been a matter of increasing consciousness: "Right at its base, the living world is constituted by consciousness clothed in flesh and bone" (p. 151). Joseph Kopp (1964), an interpreter of Teilhard de Chardin's concepts, puts it this way: "The living world consists intrinsically of consciousness clothed in flesh . . . the axis on which evolution drives ahead is of a spiritual not a material nature" (p. 36).

Wilber, Teilhard de Chardin, and many others concur that, since the outset, creation has contained all physical and spiritual matter, spirit rising out of matter in the creative act of selfexperiencing and self-discovery.

Consequently, whether we think we are dealing with matter or spirit, our expressions come from the same underlying manifestation in its continual unfolding. In fact, Teilhard de Chardin (1965) coined the term *noosphere* to describe the layer of thinking brains enveloping the planet—an enormous concentration of collective human consciousness wherein everyone influences everyone else.

Whether from indigenous sources or contemporary mystics, the portrayal of a unified cosmos increasingly comes forth. Native American Elder of the Bear Clan Lodge, Waynonaha Two Worlds (2001) tells us:

> We live on a delicate web made of the finest silk. This was woven by Grandmother Spider to hold us all together. Each one of us holds a strand of this web. What happens to one of us happens to us all from one end of this Turtle Island to the other and beyond (e-mail communication).

Carl Jung spoke to this in terms of the collective unconscious, describing how universal imprints of behavior, emotional responsiveness, and potentiality connect us. Here is where individual shadow material finds support in the collective shadow allowing expressions of racism, hatred, and righteousness to run rampant. And here, once our projections are taken back, is where we contribute to the collective experience of expansion and growth. In *Journeying*, I said it this way:

> As the energies of sublimation, altruism, suppression, anticipation, humor, and empathy come forward, they reflect a life lived through individual expression rather than collective repression. Spreading across the collective web, these energies catalyze movement toward individuation. From this perspective, the ripening of any individual would invigorate the healing of the whole of humanity. And it would defuse the powerlessness felt by people who see no means for impeding the escalation of chaos and violence in the world. Admitting to emotions that have been denied and defended against is the work of heroes and heroines, and at once an act of self-empathy and collective compassion (1998, p. 150).

The worldwide Web is a literal metaphor for our connectedness, further emphasized by the legendary tale of the hundredth monkey. The story goes like this: within a colony of monkeys, the task of learning to peel sweet potatoes was taken on. Struggling with a limited degree of manual dexterity, one by one the monkeys mastered the challenge. When the hundredth monkey put his peeled potato on the ground, the critical number had been reached. From that time forward, monkeys all over the world showed a natural facility for peeling potatoes. As far-fetched as this may sound, the ease with which children pick up technological concepts and implement new behaviors blows the minds of many an adult, causing them to wonder if the younger brains didn't arrive better equipped.

Man's journey toward oneness stretches back a million years. The search for meaning and connection, embryonic as it may have been initially, when man first looked within himself and realized he was a *somebody*, carries its own brand of evidence. One day when visiting a favorite Santa Fe shop where fetishes from Southwestern Native

American communities are sold, I happened on a quartz carving of a delicate hand with lapis fingernails, less than an inch in size. I carried this small item to the counter to inquire about its origins. "It means *we are here*," the shop owner said as she further elaborated, "It is the statement of our earliest ancestors as they stamped the imprint of their hands on cave walls and into the ground. This is how they signified their humanness to each other, and this is how the hand came to indicate unity with the fingers serving as pathways into the central palm."

It is the hand that delivers the newborn baby. It is the hand that reaches out to another for connection. It is the hand we hold over our hearts when we feel love and concern. It is the metaphorical hand that reaches for the upper stages of spiritual expansion, and it is the physical hand that touches another with healing and nurturing intent. And our path up through the stages takes both— one hand horizontally connected with humankind and the other hand vertically extended toward transcendence.

We are back to the beginning where the fullness of our humanness—the capacity to connect, nurture, and love— comes through the hands and the hearts of our caretakers and those who nurture and mentor us. We are back to the beginning of where religions have at their core the concept of love. In our advance toward the evolutionary goal of culminated consciousness and unity—what Teilhard de Chardin (1959) called *Point Omega*—his words resound: "All we may well need is to imagine our power of love developing until it embraces the total of men and of the earth" (p. 266). This is merely another way of describing how transcending the personal ego *refines the humane*, leading us into a high altitude of connection and compassion.

The implications of more and more individuals maturing their egos and living from a place of unitive consciousness are staggering. Those who *love* from the foundation of an intact ego not threatened by difference or challenges and who are able to empathically connect while remaining true to their individuality catalyze growth pursuits in others. Those whose *creativity* springs forth unfettered by greed, envy, or competition not only supply a vast array of resources to local communities but also invest energy into the resolution of societal and ecological concerns.

The journey up through the stages to this platform may seem lifelong. Yet we must not forget the acceleration of twenty-first-century change and development. With map in hand and joined by fellow travelers, with the offering of mutual assistance and the footprints of those who went before us, we quicken our steps and lighten our load. What seems a vertical ascent turns horizontal, for the journey upward is the journey inward. And here, from *within our within*, we live in the land we dream of, where ego maturity allows us to be exactly who we are meant to be, where we experience joy and love without bounds, and where hearts on fire with compassion transform the planetary soul.

WORKS CITED

Funk, J. (2000). Inspired creativity. In M. E. Miller & S. R. Cook-Greuter (Eds.), *Creativity, spirituality, and transcendence: Paths of integrity and wisdom in the mature self* (Chapter 4). New York: Elsevier Science.

Gagan, J. M. (1998). *Journeying: Where shamanism and psychology meet.* Santa Fe, NM: Rio Chama Publications.

Hall, C. & Lindzey, G. (1978). Organismic Theory. In *Theories of personality* (3rd ed. pp. 241-277). New York: John Wiley & Sons.

Kopp, J. V. (1964). *Teilhard de Chardin: A new synthesis of evolution.* Glen Rock, NJ: Deus Books. Maslow, A. H. (1970). *Motivation and personality* (2nd ed.). New York: Harper.

Maslow, A. H. (1971). *The farther reaches of human nature.* New York: Viking Press.

Teilhard de Chardin, P. (1959). *The phenomenon of man.* New York: Harper & Row.

Teilhard de Chardin, P. (1965). *Building the earth.* New York: Avon Books. Vaillant, G. E. (1993). *The wisdom of the ego.* Cambridge, MA: Harvard University Press. Waynonaha Two Worlds (2001): E-mail communication, September 3, 2001.

Wilber, K. (1998b). *The essential Ken Wilber: An introductory reader.* Boston: Shambhala.

Appendix A

Growth Spiral Images

1. Presocial
2. Symbiotic
3. Impulsive
4. Self-Protective
5. Conformist
6. Self-Aware
7. Conscientious
8. Individualistic
9. Autonomous
10. Universal/Integrated

Appendix A. Growth Spiral Images

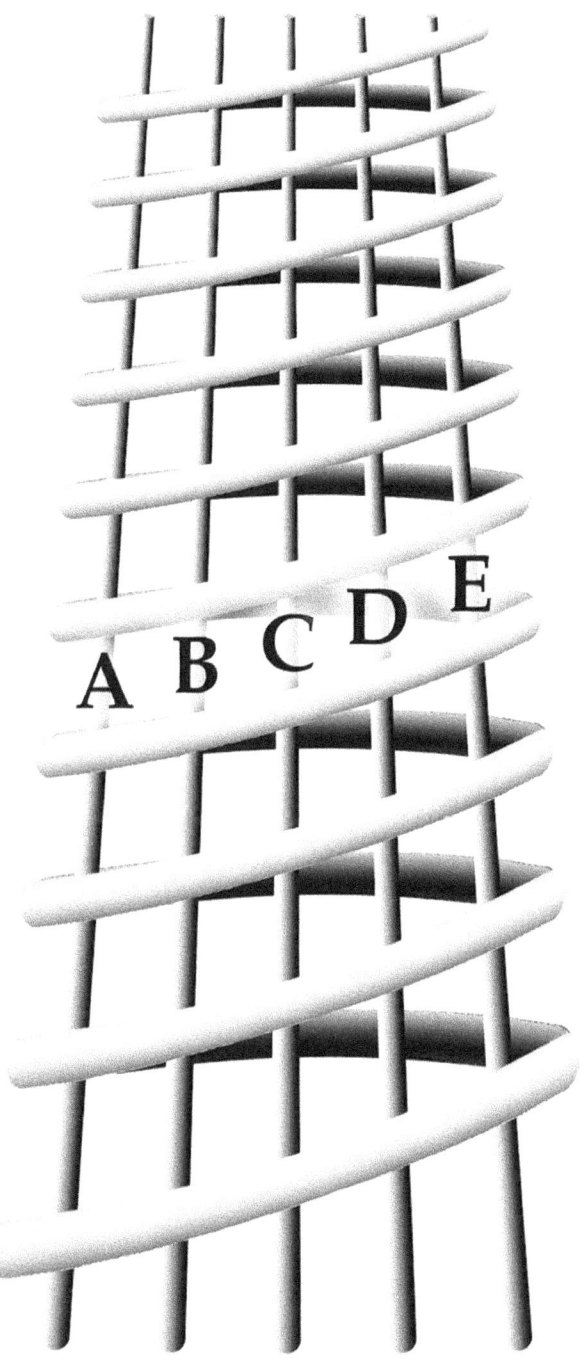

Appendix B

Feeling Word List

I feel . . .

AFFECTIONATE
compassionate
friendly
loving
open hearted
sympathetic
tender
warm

AFRAID
apprehensive
dread
foreboding
frightened
mistrustful

panicked
petrified
scared
suspicious
terrified
wary
worried

CONFUSED
ambivalent
baffled
bewildered
dazed
hesitant
lost

mystified
perplexed
puzzled
torn

ENGAGED
absorbed
alert
curious
engrossed
enchanted
entranced
fascinated
interested
intrigued
involved
spellbound
stimulated

HOPEFUL
expectant
encouraged
optimistic

CONFIDENT
empowered
open
proud
safe
secure

EXCITED
amazed
animated

ardent
aroused
astonished
dazzled
eager
energetic
enthusiastic
giddy
invigorated
lively
passionate
surprised
vibrant

GRATEFUL
appreciative
moved
thankful
touched

INSPIRED
amazed
awed
wonder

JOYFUL
amused
delighted
glad
happy
jubilant
pleased
tickled

EXHILARATED
blissful
ecstatic
elated
enthralled
exuberant
radiant
rapturous
thrilled

EMBARRASSED
ashamed
chagrined
flustered
guilty
mortified
self-conscious

FATIGUED
beat
burnt out
depleted
exhausted
lethargic
tired
weary
worn out

PEACEFUL
calm
clear headed
comfortable
centered
content
equanimous
fulfilled
mellow
quiet
relaxed
relieved
satisfied
serene
still
tranquil
trusting

TENSE
anxious
cranky
distressed
distraught
edgy
fidgety
frazzled
irritable
jittery
nervous
overwhelmed
restless
stressed out

REFRESHED
enlivened
rejuvenated
renewed
rested
restored
revived

ANNOYED
aggravated
dismayed
disgruntled
displeased
exasperated
frustrated
impatient
irritated
irked

ANGRY
enraged
furious
incensed
indignant
irate
livid
outraged
resentful

AVERSION
animosity
appalled
contempt
disgusted
dislike
hate
horrified
hostile
repulsed

DISCONNECTED
alienated
aloof
apathetic
bored
cold
detached
distant
distracted
indifferent
numb
removed
uninterested
withdrawn

YEARNING
envious
jealous
longing
nostalgic
pining
wistful

DISQUIETED
agitated
alarmed
discombobulated
disconcerted
disconnected
disturbed
perturbed
rattled
restless
shocked

startled
surprised
troubled
turbulent
uncomfortable
uneasy
unnerved
unsettled
upset

VULNERABLE
fragile
guarded
helpless
insecure
leery
reserved
sensitive shaky

Copyright © 2005 Center for Nonviolent Communication, www.cnvc.org; used with permission.

Appendix C

Professional Help

Resources

1. Ask trusted friends, family, clergy, or a family physician about professionals they may know.

2. Call your local community health center or a university/college counseling center.

3. Call your health insurance company for a mental health provider list.

4. Use referral listings from national professional psychotherapists organizations, such as:

   - American Psychological Association www.apa.org
   - American Social Workers Association www.socialworkers.org
   - American Mental Health Counseling Association www.amhca.org
   - Eye Movement Desensitization and Reprocessing Therapists www.emdr.com
   - Developmental Needs Meeting Strategy Therapists www.dnmsinstitute.com

www.ingramcontent.com/pod-product-compliance
Lightning Source LLC
Chambersburg PA
CBHW080549030426
42337CB00024B/4817